The Association for Asian Studies

Occasional Papers, Number 1

Edgar Wickberg, *Editor*

The Association
for Asian Studies

AN INTERPRETIVE HISTORY

CHARLES O. HUCKER

Published for the Association for Asian Studies
by the UNIVERSITY OF WASHINGTON PRESS
Seattle and London

First Edition, 1973

Printed in the United States of America

Library of Congress Cataloging in Publication Data

Hucker, Charles O
   The Association for Asian Studies.

   (Association for Asian Studies. Occasional
papers, no. 1)
   Bibliography: p.
   1. Association for Asian Studies--History.
I. Series.
DS1.A7854   915'.006'273   72-13474
ISBN 0-295-95266-0 (pbk)

FOREWORD

This volume is the first in a new series to be called the Occasional Papers of the Association for Asian Studies. The purpose of the series is to accommodate types of manuscripts that fit into neither of the two existing series sponsored by the Association, the Monographs Series and the Reference Series. The range in size and subject matter of manuscripts suitable to the new Occasional Papers series can be as broad as the imagination and judgment of contributors and editors may dictate.

The publication of Charles Hucker's interpretive history of the AAS makes generally available for the first time a record of the first twenty years' history of the world's largest association devoted to the scholarly study of eastern and southern Asia, together with the interesting interpretations of an informed participant in that history. As the author points out in his Preface, this is a personal interpretation, not an "official" history of the Association. Its publication by the AAS does not imply endorsement of either the author's selection of material or his interpretation of it.

Edgar Wickberg, Editor
Monographs, Occasional Papers,
and Reference Series, AAS

PREFACE

This history was written during the winter of
1969/70 in fulfillment of an obligation undertaken by the Association for Asian Studies to
contribute an analysis of itself to a broad-
ranging evaluation of foreign language and
area studies in America that was then being
conducted by Professor Richard D. Lambert under
contract with the U.S. Office of Education. It
is published now in the present format, without
any emendations except for minor editorial tidy-
ing-up, because officers of the Association
believe it may be of interest to members and
other readers. However, it should not be considered an official history of the Association.
The officers and the Board of Directors of the
Association neither approve nor disapprove the
presentation, but quite properly consider it my
own highly personal interpretation.
    The history was written by me only because I
allowed myself to be persuaded that I might
approach the task with a desirable combination
of familiarity and detachment, being a long-time
member, a one-time director, and most particularly the immediate past secretary of the
Association. There is unlikely to be general
agreement that I have achieved a wholly balanced,
wholly informed, and wholly judicious presenta-

tion. But I have tried to be honest and fair, neither glossing over unpleasant memories that some members would prefer to leave dormant nor indulging in muck-raking gossip that some members would relish.

The factual substance of the history is derived primarily from the files of the Association's Secretariat in Ann Arbor, to which my research assistant, Arne de Keijzer, and I were granted free access. Several persons who have been involved in the Association's affairs long and intimately helped by answering questions patiently or by offering criticisms of the first draft. Consequently, although I cannot presume to have risen far beyond the limitations imposed by my own experiences and interests, I am confident that the history is factually accurate and does not, by inappropriate selections and omissions of data, grossly distort what has happened to the Association and why. The presentation was shaped in some measure by analytical guidelines prescribed by Professor Lambert. Nevertheless, I accept full personal responsibility for decisions about selection of the analytical themes that are pursued and the differing emphases that are given them, as well as for the opinions and interpretations that are offered.

Charles O. Hucker

Ann Arbor, Michigan
July, 1972

CONTENTS

The Association for Asian Studies

An Interpretive History

INTRODUCTION

The Association for Asian Studies is the world's
largest and most active learned society devoted
to promoting interest in and the scholarly study
of all aspects of the cultures and civilizations
of East, Southeast, South, and Inner Asia. It
is a nonprofit, tax-exempt association incorporated in the state of New York, with a Secretariat
located in Ann Arbor, Michigan, that serves as
its principal administrative headquarters and
with a current dues-paying membership of 4,700.
It convenes an annual national meeting every
March or April that in recent years has been
normally attended by between 1,500 and 2,000 registered participants, and it shares in sponsoring
six annual regional conferences. It publishes a
quarterly *Journal of Asian Studies* distributed
to more than seven thousand members and subscribers, an annual *Bibliography of Asian Studies,* a
quarterly *Newsletter,* and an irregular Monographs
and Papers series.

   Until 1956 the Association was known as the
Far Eastern Association, Inc., and its journal
was called *The Far Eastern Quarterly;* formally
defined areas of interest did not include South
Asia (present India, Ceylon, Pakistan, etc.).
The Far Eastern Association originated as an
organized membership society in 1948, after

having existed since 1941 as a nonmembership corporation for the sole purpose of publishing *The Far Eastern Quarterly*.

The presentation and interpretation of the history of the Association for Asian Studies that follows is an independent undertaking by the author under the Association's sponsorship and is based upon free access to all of the Association's official files. It owes much to the research assistance of Arne de Keijzer of Ann Arbor.

GENERAL HISTORICAL BACKGROUND

Organized scholarship on Asia in America began
in 1842 with the founding of the American Oriental Society, which remained the only learned
society serving the interests of American students of Asia until 1948. From the beginning,
the Society's publications and activities reflected a predominant interest in Biblical studies
and related studies of the ancient civilizations
of Egypt and Mesopotamia. Islamic and Sanskritic
studies, and to a much lesser extent studies of
ancient Chinese civilization, had come within the
Society's sphere of interest by the end of the
nineteenth century; and in the twentieth century
the Society gradually developed interests in
Persian, Turkic, and other realms of what is now
generally known as the Middle East, as well as
in Japanese studies. But the Society's focus remained predominantly philological and premodern,
as it does today.
   Meanwhile, and especially during the years between the First and Second World Wars, both popular and academic interest in all parts of Asia
grew slowly in America. Areas in which Americans
had substantial political and cultural involvements, i.e., East and Southeast Asia, were empha-
sized; areas under British dominion, i.e., South
Asia, were de-emphasized. In academic realms,

leadership and financial support came primarily from the American Council of Learned Societies and the Rockefeller Foundation, under whose auspices a succession of promising young American scholars went to Asia for field experience, especially in China, in some instances undertook advanced study in those university centers in Europe that had relatively long traditions of Asian scholarship, and on their return found teaching positions in leading American universities. A few American universities also took notable initiatives in developing Asian studies, Harvard first with establishment of the Harvard-Yenching Institute in 1930. In non-academic realms, leadership was taken by political-education organizations such as the Foreign Policy Association and, most particularly, the Institute of Pacific Relations. The Institute of Pacific Relations existed until 1961 as an international organization, the American branch of which was established in New York in 1925 and published the periodicals *Pacific Affairs* and *Far Eastern Survey* (both continued since 1961 under other auspices).

The Second World War dramatically accelerated American involvements with Asia on many planes, not least of which was the academic. Most young Asian studies specialists were swept up at least temporarily, and often for continuing careers, in government service, to apply their specialized knowledge and skills to war problems either in Washington or in the field overseas. Hundreds of young servicemen were given intensive training in Asian languages, especially Chinese and Japanese, and sent as interpreters and intelligence officers into East Asia. Of these, and of the hundreds of thousands of other Americans who experienced military service in Asia during the war, a small proportion dedicated themselves to preparation for scholarly careers in Asian studies at the end of the war. Although they

6

were few in absolute numbers, they were unprece-
dentedly numerous in light of the educational
programs that existed to absorb them; and both
public and academic opinion now recognized the
legitimate and necessary role of Asian studies
in American education, at least to a degree un-
dreamed of earlier. After 1945, consequently,
academic programs in Asian studies, and especially East Asian (i.e., Far Eastern) studies,
steadily multiplied.

The development of American scholarship on
Asia in the years following the Second World War
was influenced by a number of new factors. Contemporary history was fascinating and controversial. Americans occupied and governed Japan
until 1952. China agonized through a civil war
that had specially controversial political ramifications in America and culminated in a Chinese
Communist takeover of the mainland in 1949.
Local independence movements emerged elsewhere,
especially in French Indo-China, the Philippines,
the Netherlands East Indies, and South Asian
portions of the British Empire. Many Americans
who had served in these areas during the war and
others whose interest in Asia developed in such
times were understandably most concerned about
the modern and contemporary situation; and their
emergence on the academic scene coincided with a
growing awareness of the importance of Asia
within the social science disciplines that focus
principally on contemporary problems--political
science most notably, and economics, sociology,
and anthropology more slowly. At the same time
many Americans who were now interested in Asia,
without necessarily being indifferent to contemporary political and social problems there, were
attracted to varied aspects of the Asian cultures
--languages and literatures, thought and relig-
ions, art and music. Asian studies therefore began to penetrate all of the traditional humanistic and social science disciplines and could no

7

longer be confined to exotic and esoteric lagoons away from the academic mainstream.

Acceptance of Asian specialists in some disciplines came slowly, nevertheless; and in many disciplines they felt themselves isolated in some degree both from their fellow disciplinarians who had no special interest in Asia and from their Asian-specialist counterparts in other disciplines. There was consequently a growing need for an area-oriented organization on a national scale that could serve as a rallying point for all Asian specialists and could provide the services and support they wanted. For some, the American Oriental Society served this purpose quite satisfactorily, but the Society's traditional philological and premodern emphases made it an unsatisfactory outlet for and supporter of the interests of many others. For some, the Institute of Pacific Relations served the purpose satisfactorily, but the Institute was never a membership-type learned society, and in any event its emphasis on political education made it unappealing to many Asian studies scholars.

EMERGENCE OF THE FAR EASTERN ASSOCIATION

The feeling of need for a different sort of learned society in the Asian studies field was not entirely a new, postwar phenomenon. Some steps to provide needed services had been taken even before the war, chiefly with the encouragement and partial financial support of the American Council of Learned Societies. Publication of a *Bulletin of Far Eastern Bibliography* in a very simple format began in 1936 and continued through five volumes by the end of 1940, under the editorship of Earl H. Pritchard. In 1941 Pritchard and Cyrus H. Peake, both then at Columbia University, decided in consultation with their Columbia colleague Hugh Borton to expand the *Bulletin* into a more rounded journal. Toward this end they sought and received support from Asian specialists at several other institutions, and on June 9, 1941, the enlarged group officially organized itself as The Far Eastern Association, a nonprofit organization incorporated under the Membership Corporation Law of the State of New York. Its members and directors, in addition to Borton, Peake, and Pritchard, were Knight Biggerstaff of Cornell, Woodbridge Bingham of Berkeley, Harley Farnsworth MacNair of Chicago, and Karl August Wittfogel of New York City. The sole purpose of the Association so constituted

9

was to sponsor publication of *The Far Eastern Quarterly*. Borton, Peake, and Pritchard undertook to serve as editors of the journal. Peake, as Managing Editor, took general responsibility for soliciting and editing articles and for financial management, and Pritchard assumed responsibility for soliciting book reviews and for preparing regular bibliographic sections that now replaced the abandoned *Bulletin*. An Advisory Editorial Board was organized to include, in addition to the directors already named, William B. Ballis, Meribeth E. Cameron, Kenneth W. Colegrove, George B. Cressey, Charles B. Fahs, John K. Fairbank, Robert B. Hall, Harold J. Noble, Harold S. Quigley, Frederic D. Schultheis, Earl Swisher, and Virginia Thompson. In 1942-43 Amry Vandenbosch and Edwin G. Beal, Jr., were added. The first issue of *The Far Eastern Quarterly* appeared in November, 1941.

During the war years that immediately followed Borton, Peake, and Pritchard all engaged in government service in Washington but managed nevertheless to continue publishing the *Quarterly*. At the end of the war in 1945 the editorial triumvirate scattered, Borton returning to Columbia, Peake being assigned to government duty in Japan, and Pritchard going to what is now Wayne State University in Detroit. Pritchard assumed the responsibility of Managing Editor. By November 1947 Pritchard as Editor, by then having moved to Chicago, was assisted by Borton of Columbia, Cecil Hobbs of the Library of Congress, Lauriston Sharp of Cornell, Bingham of Berkeley (preparing Notes and News sections), Meribeth E. Cameron of Milwaukee-Downer College (editing book reviews), and Gussie E. Gaskill of Cornell (compiling Far Eastern Bibliography sections). Colegrove of Northwestern, Cressey of Syracuse, Fairbank of Harvard, Hall of Michigan, Noble of Oregon, Peake (now back in Washington), Quigley of Minnesota, Schultheis of Washington, Swisher of Colorado,

Virginia Thompson of the Institute of Pacific Relations, Vandenbosch of Kentucky, and Wittfogel of the Institute of Social Research remained on the Advisory Editorial Board, newly supplemented by George M. McCune of Berkeley, Harriet L. Moore of the American Russian Institute, and Edwin O. Reischauer of Harvard.

Long before 1948, however, the Association and its *Quarterly* were in serious financial difficulties, for the publication had never become self-supporting. No sustained effort had been made to solicit advertising, and none seemed promising. A trickle of advertising income combined with subscription fees left the *Quarterly* with a deficit of hundreds of dollars every year. All that kept the publication alive was the dedication of its editorial staff and, from the beginning, a continuing series of financial contributions from Norman Dwight Harris of Evanston, Illinois, which in effect regularly made up the *Quarterly*'s deficits. Increased income was clearly necessary to perpetuate the effort.

Meanwhile, since the end of the Second World War, a Committee on Far Eastern Studies, constituted and supported by the American Council of Learned Societies and chaired by Knight Biggerstaff of Cornell, had been considering ways of fostering scholarship in the field and increasingly noted the scholarly value and potential of the *Quarterly* as well as its fiscal difficulties. At a special meeting in Washington on January 3, 1948, the Committee and some nonmember invited guests discussed the possibility of establishing an active membership organization to serve a number of needs including sponsorship of the *Quarterly*. Those attending were Chairman Biggerstaff, Bingham of Berkeley, Borton of Columbia, Herrlee G. Creel of Chicago, Charles B. Fahs of the Rockefeller Foundation, Fairbank of Harvard, Clarence H. Hamilton of Oberlin, William W. Lockwood of Princeton, Laurence S. C. Sickman of the

11

Nelson Gallery of Art in Kansas City, and Joseph K. Yamagiwa of Michigan. This group authorized an effort to organize a learned society called The Far Eastern Association and constituted a planning committee of three--Bingham, Pritchard, and Reischauer--to arrange an organizational meeting in the near future. In doing this, the planning committee obtained help and advice from members of the larger group named above, from the editors of the *Quarterly*, from representatives of the Southeast Asia Institute (an organization that had emerged during the war along the organizational lines of the Institute of Pacific Relations), and from a New York City attorney, Jonathan Bingham, as legal counselor.

The organizational meeting was planned quickly and was held on the Columbia University campus in New York on April 2, 1948, with Biggerstaff serving as temporary chairman and John A. Pope of the Freer Gallery of Art in Washington serving as temporary secretary. What was hailed as a propitiously large turnout of between 175 and 200 persons attended. The meeting was not without controversial discussion: It was proposed that membership be restricted to scholars; there was extended discussion about the proposed association's possible sponsorship of closed meetings of scholarly specialists as well as general open meetings; there were questions about the relationship between the proposed association and the Institute of Pacific Relations, which had recently been included in (though it was subsequently removed from) a list of subversive organizations published by the state of California. But without much hesitation participants in the meeting agreed to organize themselves formally as The Far Eastern Association. They elected Arthur W. Hummel of the Library of Congress as President for a one-year term, Robert B. Hall of Michigan as Vice-President for a one-year term, and a board of nine Directors for staggered terms of

12

one, two, and three years: Lockwood of Princeton, James M. Menzies of Cheloo University (in China), and George E. Taylor of Washington for one year; Bingham of Berkeley, Pope of the Freer Gallery, and C. Martin Wilbur of Columbia for two years; and Raymond Kennedy of Yale, Virginia Thompson of the Institute of Pacific Relations, and Ssu-yü Teng of Chicago for three years.

A Constitution and By-laws had been drafted by Pritchard in consultation with his colleagues on the planning committee, and they were adopted with minor revisions, stating the objectives of the Association as follows:

The objectives of the Association shall be: (a) to form a scholarly, nonpolitical, and nonprofit professional association of all persons interested in the study of the Far East; (b) to promote interest in and scholarly study of the Far East; (c) to provide means for the publication of scholarly research and other materials designed to promote Far Eastern studies; (d) to promote co-operative activities and exchange of information within the field of Far Eastern studies in the United States and Canada; and (e) to facilitate contact and exchange of information between scholars and scholarly organizations in the United States and Canada interested in Far Eastern studies and those in other countries.

The Constitution provided that the President and Vice-President of the Association should join the nine elected Directors in constituting the Board of Directors, and that the two immediate past Presidents as well as appointed officers-- a Secretary or Executive Secretary, a Treasurer, and the editors of Association publications-- should participate in meetings of the Board. The Constitution called for an annual membership

13

meeting of the Association, comprising a business session and a planned program of papers and discussions; and By-laws provided that *The Far Eastern Quarterly* should be the official journal of the Association and that the Association should endeavor to publish a Monograph Series. By-laws set membership dues at $6 per year. It was also prescribed that:

> In preparing the list of nominees for the Board of Directors the (Nominating) Committee shall keep in mind the desirability of having representation on the Board from the various sections of the country as well as scholars representing interest in the several regions of the Far East and the various disciplines engaged in Far Eastern study.

Whereas the By-laws originally drafted by the planning committee anticipated that the Vice-President should normally be nominated for President the following year, the By-laws that were adopted prescribed the reverse: "The nominee for President shall normally not be the Vice-President of the preceding year." This change was the result of persuasive arguments, chiefly by Charles Sidney Gardner of Cambridge, Massachusetts, about regrettable experiences in other learned societies with virtually automatic succession to the presidency by the Vice-President. Nothing in the Constitution or By-laws specifically defined the Association's geographic area of interest more narrowly than "the Far East," but the Principles of Editorial Policy published in volume VII, number 4 (August, 1948) of the *Quarterly* stated that "Articles will be divided as evenly as possible between Southeast Asia, China, and Japan and Northeast Asia . . ." That Southeast Asia would be well represented in the Association was assured when the Southeast

Asia Institute dissolved itself in June, 1948, and urged its members to join the new Association, as many did.

At the close of the organizational meeting the newly elected Board of Directors appointed Wilma Fairbank Secretary, Hugh Borton Treasurer, Earl H. Pritchard Editor of the *Quarterly*, and John K. Fairbank Editor of the proposed Monograph Series. A membership list was published in volume VIII, number 2 (February, 1949) of the *Quarterly*, identifying 512 regular members, 29 associate members (spouses of other members, paying $1 dues), 26 supporting members (contributors of $10 per year), one patron (Norman Dwight Harris), and five sponsoring or supporting institutions: The University of California at Berkeley, the University of Chicago, Cornell University, the University of Hawaii Library, and Mount Holyoke College.

The first membership meeting of the new Association was held at Yale University over three days in early April, 1949, as a joint meeting with the American Oriental Society. A program of papers was offered, organized by a program committee under the chairmanship of Raymond Kennedy of Yale. The business meeting was informed that current membership had reached a total of 606 and that there currently were 63 nonmember individual subscribers and 460 institutional subscribers to the *Quarterly*. A Nominating Committee chaired by L. Carrington Goodrich of Columbia and including Creel of Chicago, Allan Cole of Pomona, Shannon McCune of Colgate, and Lloyd S. Millegan of the Department of State had prepared a slate of nominees for mail balloting. As a result of this Charles Sidney Gardner became the new President, Virginia Thompson Adloff was elected the new Vice-President of the Association, and William L. Holland of the Institute of Pacific Relations, Owen Lattimore of Johns Hopkins, Reischauer of Harvard, and George Cressey of Syracuse became new members of the Board of Directors, the latter filling the unexpired term of the newly elected Vice-President, Mrs. Adloff.

During its meeting at Yale the Board of Directors reached two important policy decisions. On one hand, it agreed that:

Whereas it might be useful to meet with the AOS (i.e. the American Oriental Society) when mutually convenient, we need not have a policy of meeting with them always. In fact it would be more advantageous for us to cover leading centers of Far Eastern studies in our first years. . . .

On the other hand, the Board agreed upon a governing principle for the Nominating Committee regarding the presidency of the Association:

1) The presidency should be considered as an honor paid to outstanding scholars and as such should always go to the eminent older scholars. 2) It should alternate as much as possible on the one hand between scholars representing the humanities and the social sciences and on the other between scholars primarily interested in China, Northeast Asia (Japan, Korea, Soviet Far East, Mongolia), and Southeast Asia. 3) The office should also alternate between the different regions of the U.S. as much as circumstances will permit.

THE ERA OF CONSOLIDATION,
1949-1955

Once it had become a membership organization,
the Far Eastern Association rapidly attained organizational stability and general recognition as
a learned society. Membership grew slowly,
reaching a total of 734 in spring 1955, by which
time nonmember subscriptions had grown at a con-
siderably faster rate to 929. Revenues increased
from approximately $8,500 in 1949 to approxi-
mately $14,500 in 1955; and, although expenses
exceeded revenues in three of these seven calendar years, the Association's solvency was
assured. The *Quarterly* maintained its publication schedule and grew slightly in total pages
published annually. Gifts from Mr. and Mrs.
Richard Adloff and allocations from the Association's general funds made possible publication
of the first two titles in the Monograph Series,
Delmer M. Brown's *Money Economy in Medieval
Japan* and Earl Swisher's *China's Management of
the American Barbarians,* both in 1951; and a
grant of $10,000 in 1955 by the Council on Eco-
nomic and Cultural Affairs specifically for this
purpose assured continuation of the series.
Membership meetings were held annually in late
March or early April, jointly with the Association of American Geographers in 1953. The
original pattern of three-day annual meetings

17

continued uninterrupted; by 1955 the program had expanded to include 22 panels of papers and discussions, and arrangements with the United States Employment Service provided job placement opportunities for the membership. Beginning in 1952 a succession of Association Secretaries affiliated with the University of Michigan had firmly rooted the Association's secretarial activities in Ann Arbor. In 1955 the Board of Directors authorized the establishment there of a permanent Secretariat, with a partial subvention from the University's Center for Japanese Studies and with the assistance of a Manager on three-quarter time service, Mrs. Victoria Harper (later to become Mrs. Spang). In 1952 the Association initiated a request for acceptance as one of the constituent member societies of the American Council of Learned Societies, and its membership was approved effective January 10, 1954.

No major organizational changes were made during these years. In 1952 the Board of Directors proposed, and the general membership later approved, changing the By-laws pertaining to the presidency to read "The nominee for President shall normally be the Vice-President of the preceding year," thus reversing the position taken by the organizational meeting in 1949 and restoring the intent of the original draft Constitution and By-laws prepared by the planning committee for that meeting. As regards annual meetings, the Board in 1954 decided that joint meetings with the American Oriental Society were useful but should not be scheduled oftener than every other year. Regarding finances, the Board in 1953 authorized depositing Association funds in savings and loan associations in the hope of obtaining better returns than the 1.9% currently earned on its bank deposits and for the first time authorized the allocation of funds to support editorial preparation of the Far Eastern

Bibliography section of the *Quarterly*. In 1954 the Board authorized an increase from $500 to $550 in annual expenditures by the Secretary, the selling of advertising space in the program of the annual meeting, and the recruitment of a volunteer advertising manager to try to increase revenues from advertisements in the *Quarterly*. In 1955 membership dues were increased from $6 to $7, the preparation of a regular annual budget was prescribed for the first time, and a Research Committee on Development of Far Eastern Studies was created, with Hugh Borton as its chairman, for the purpose of exploring possibilities of foundation support for expanding Association activities and services.

In these years of organizational consolidation the Association repeatedly felt threatened by political entanglements, especially those growing out of the emergence of a Communist government in mainland China and American reactions to it, and most particularly Congressional investigations into the activities of the Institute of Pacific Relations, with which many Association members had long had close ties as individuals. This aspect of the Association's history will be fully considered in subsequent pages. Here it may suffice to remark that by 1955 the Association had survived these difficult times without incurring any stigma as an organization but that some of its members survived with scars, antagonisms, or fears and the Association's leadership on the whole was increasingly dedicated to keeping the Association unambiguously out of politics.

Although the Association achieved and maintained fiscal soundness and stability in this era, it was apparent by 1955 that the Association needed increased revenues, which it could hope to obtain only from outside sources such as the newly created Ford Foundation, if it were to fulfill the mission it had accepted to promote Far Eastern scholarship.

As early as December, 1949, at a special
meeting in Cambridge, Massachusetts, the Board of
Directors had taken responsibility to seek new
funding and had set the following priorities for
the use of such funds as were available or could
be obtained: (1) publication of research, (2) the
maintenance of an effective Secretariat, (3)
scholarships and fellowships, and (4) summer institutes on Far Eastern studies for nonspecialist
teachers. A year before, on December 10, 1948,
the officers and Directors of the new Association
had met jointly with the Committee on Far Eastern
Studies of the American Council of Learned Societies and had formed a joint Policy Committee
charged with considering the state of the profession and recommending ways in which Far Eastern studies might be further fostered. The
Policy Committee, chaired by Hugh Borton, called
for reports from several subcommittees: One concerned with translations of Chinese dynastic
histories, one on publications (Joseph K.
Yamagiwa and John K. Fairbank), one on regional
conferences and institutes (Paul H. Clyde, Chairman; Virginia Thompson Adloff, Shannon McCune,
and Joseph K. Yamagiwa), and one on the development of instructional materials (Harold E.
Shadick and Richard Beardsley. The Policy Committee itself met at Columbia University on
January 25, 1949; again on April 4 at Yale University; and finally in Chicago on May 28, 29,
and 30. At that time it formulated a report entitled "A Program for the Promotion of Far
Eastern Studies in the United States." As regards placement of personnel, the Policy Committee reported:

There are signs that the production of
specialists in the Far Eastern field is
catching up with the immediate demand.
Wartime language training programs in
Japanese and Chinese and wartime interest

in the Far East brought a large number of highly talented students into the field, and, as the first members of this group won their Ph.D. degrees, they have quickly filled the demand for teachers which had piled up during the war and first post-war years. We may soon be faced with the situation of having good young scholars with their degrees (but) without positions. The continuance of the training program at or near present numerical levels, though essential if we are to build up our knowledge of the Far East, is not justifiable in human terms unless suitable positions can be found for the younger scholars in the field.

This Committee believes that, although we are beginning to meet immediate demands for scholars in our field, we are very far from meeting the potential demand. A large proportion of the colleges and universities of the United States are without instruction of any sort in the Far Eastern field, and many others, though having the Far East in their curriculum, do not have specially trained instructors for this work. We will not have met the potential demand for scholars in our field until every institution of higher learning has specially trained scholars in the Far Eastern field.

The Policy Committee also recommended that the Committee on Far Eastern Studies of the American Council of Learned Societies remain in existence and that it should:

1. Constantly evaluate and survey Far Eastern studies in the United States and give serious consideration to plans for their development.

2. Make recommendations on broad fields of research which should be undertaken, including plans as to how such research can be carried out.

3. Develop plans and make recommendations on projects which do not properly belong to any other agency and which arise out of the context of serious planning reconsideration. Projects in this category which had already been undertaken by the Committee and which are continuing include the "Chinese Translation Project" and the revision of the "Selected List of Books and Articles on Japan." New projects which should receive immediate consideration of the Committee include:

    a. The means whereby the material in Washington from the International War Crimes Tribunal and the Japanese Army and Navy Department files can be most effectively used,

    b. Translation projects of materials in Chinese and Japanese,

    c. Problems connected with the acquisition or reproduction of important Chinese and Japanese material difficult to obtain because of present conditions in the Far East,

    d. The question of support of Chinese scholars who are forced to leave their country or cease scholarly activity because of political conditions and the best method whereby Chinese studies may be continued during the next few years, and

    e. Steps which should be taken to permit the exchange of Japanese and American scholars between Japan and the United States.

4. Act as a coordinating agency for various aspects of Far Eastern studies in the United States, including recommendations as to how existing organizations such as the FEA, the AOS, or the universities can assume responsibility for specific projects.
5. Offer advice to the ACLS on matters referred to the Committee by the Council.

Assignment of such responsibilities to the Committee on Far Eastern Studies, the Policy Committee suggested, would enable the Far Eastern Association "to devote its energies toward":

1. The publication of the *Far Eastern Quarterly* and the *Far Eastern Bibliography*.
2. The development of a Monograph Series, including experimentation in the most advantageous method of reproduction of volumes for this series and the examination of manuscripts presented for publication.
3. Dissemination by the FEA Secretary of information concerning Far Eastern studies in the United States.
4. Assisting universities, through the services of its Secretary, in the organization of summer institutes. . . .
5. Coordinating, through its Secretary, Far Eastern scholarly activities with governmental and non-governmental institutions as well as with foreign scholars and institutes.

At its December, 1949, meeting the Board of Directors had formally approved such a division of responsibilities between the Association and the Committee on Far Eastern Studies of the American Council of Learned Societies.

Thus, by 1955 the Association could feel it

was fulfilling some of its responsibilities in at least minimal fashion, but the existing resources were taxed to their limits so that there was little hope of providing new services. Meanwhile, the old ACLS Committee on Far Eastern Studies had become inactive for want of funds; the Association's new Research Committee on Development of Far Eastern Studies, it was hoped, might find ways to carry on the old committee's functions.

In sum, by 1955 Far Eastern studies generally and the Association in particular had attained a plateau in development. New needs were clearly felt, but the profession and the Association had no choice but to wait for new sources of financial support to appear. It was hoped that the new Ford Foundation would fund new initiatives and thus foster new development.

THE ERA OF GROWTH AND EXPANSION, 1956-1968

In 1956 the Far Eastern Association became the Association for Asian Studies, the *Far Eastern Quarterly* became the *Journal of Asian Studies*, and the Constitution and By-laws were amended to incorporate South Asia into the sphere of the Association's interest and activity. The most important organizational change was an increase in the number of elected Directors from nine to twelve, intended to provide three regular seats on the Board for South Asian specialists.

American interest in the Indian subcontinent grew significantly after British imperial control there was relinquished in 1947, and on several occasions beginning in 1951 the Association's Board of Directors had considered including South Asia within its sphere, principally on the urging of Derk Bodde of Pennsylvania. By the mid-1950s there was a substantial group of South Asian specialists in American academic institutions who felt, as many Association members had earlier felt, that the American Oriental Society did not adequately serve their organizational needs. At the 1955 Board meeting three such specialists-- Richard Lambert, Richard L. Park, and Phillips Talbot--reported that a questionnaire distributed to South Asian specialists throughout the country had elicited responses from 150 persons, two-thirds of whom "felt that there was a mutuality of interest with the Far Eastern Association" and hoped to be given status as a "semiautonomous body" within it. The Board approved inviting such specialists to join the Association and authorized the establishment of a Committee on South Asia, which might issue a separate newsletter and take other actions to serve the special interests of the new group. At its 1956 meeting the Board authorized polling the membership for approval of the amendments in the Constitution and By-laws that formally acknowledged the newly expanded concerns of the Association.

The Association did not welcome South Asia into its realm of responsibility entirely without misgivings, and some East Asian specialists have habitually grumbled about the extent to which South Asia came to be represented in the Association's meetings, publications, committee structure, and leadership. But reaction in 1955-56 to the expansion of the Association into South Asian fields was overwhelmingly favorable. In part this reflected feelings within the Association that its responsibility for helping to promote South Asian studies was inescapable and that it owed fraternal help to the South Asian specialists. Also, there were hard practical considerations. Inclusion of South Asia appeared to be the only way to achieve an immediate increase in memberships. Moreover, since the South Asian specialists seemed prepared to set up their own organization if need be, it was felt that such agencies as the Ford Foundation would be likely to be more responsive to appeals from one organization representing the whole of Asia than from two, each with an expensive administrative-secretarial-publications structure.

Membership in the Association did indeed experience its sharpest increase to date from 1955 to 1956, rising from 763 to 903; and the 1956 total included 106 members identifiable as South Asian specialists. Moreover, favorable action regarding South Asia by the Board of Directors in 1955 did facilitate negotiations between the Association's Research Committee on Development of Far Eastern Studies and the Ford Foundation. By the end of 1955 the Ford Foundation had given the Association substantial funding of the sort required to stimulate and expand its activities.

Ford Foundation contributions in 1955 took two forms. One was a grant of $12,500 specifically to support expansion of the *Journal*, including publication of the *Bibliography of Asian Studies* (formerly the Far Eastern Bibliography section of the *Quarterly*) as a separate, fifth issue each year. (The publication of such a separate bibliography began with a September, 1955, issue of the *Quarterly*.) Another Ford grant of $38,500 included $10,000 earmarked to support the Monograph Series (supplementing the $10,000 already granted for that purpose by the Council on Economic and Cultural Affairs); the remainder of $28,500 was for general maintenance of the Secretariat, for publication of newsletters, for editorial services required by the Monograph Series, and for support of committee activities. These Ford grants were intended to support Association expansion to a new level of activity and stability by 1960. Thus in 1956 the Association had a new name, a forward-looking posture, and solid funding at least for the period immediately ahead.

Two subsequent grants from the Ford Foundation, one of $165,000 for the period 1961-65 and another of $180,000 for the period 1966-71, enabled the Association to continue and expand its essential services, to foster a variety of committees devoted to developmental projects, and to take some developmental initiatives of general sorts. Moreover, increases in membership dues from $7 to $10 in 1958 and from $10 to $15 in

1964, a fourfold growth of the membership from
903 in 1956 to 3,752 in 1968, and a steady increase of nonmembership income (nonmember subscriptions, advertising, interest on investments,
annual meeting revenues, etc.) from a total of
$13,000 in 1956 to just short of $78,000 in 1968
assured stable continued funding of the Association's basic operations and by the end of 1968
built up a cumulative reserve or equity of
$151,966.96.

Services provided by the Association from 1956
through 1968 expanded proportionately. The
Journal, continuing to appear regularly, expanded
its area coverage to include South Asia, and grew
in bulk from 658 pages in volume XV (1955-56) to
927 pages in volume XXVII (1967-68) despite rising publication costs and despite condensing its
book reviews section into small-type double col-
umns beginning in 1958. That editing the *Journal*
was a heavy burden of service deserving a stipend
was recognized in principle by the Board of Directors repeatedly in the early 1960s, and in fall
1963 it authorized a regular annual payment to
the Editor of $1,500 in the form of a summer sti-
pend. The *Bibliography* grew from 111 pages in
1955 to 456 pages in 1968. The Monograph Series,
dormant after 1951 for lack of funds, began publishing again in 1957 and published twenty-three
new titles (numbers 3-24 and 26) by the end of
1968. The *Newsletter of the Association for
Asian Studies*, inaugurated in 1955 as a four-page
folded sheet, absorbed a separate *Newsletter of
the Committee on South Asia* and became a bound
pamphlet in late 1961. By 1968 it was issued
quarterly as a bound pamphlet ranging from 56 to
nearly 100 pages per issue and it had published
extra issues on special topics in 1963, 1964,
1966, and 1967.

Annual meetings grew from a 1955 program of 22
panels of papers and discussions with approximately 500 persons in attendance to a 1968

program of 44 panels of papers and discussions with approximately 1,800 registered attendees. The annual meeting had not been held in university facilities since 1952 at Harvard. Growth of the membership in all regions of the country brought swelling demands for regular meetings west of the Alleghenies by the late 1950s. In 1961 the meeting was held at Chicago and it was decided that Chicago must be included in the regular rotation of meeting places. Later it was similarly decided that a meeting place on the West Coast must be included, beginning with a 1965 meeting in San Francisco. By 1968 it was apparent that hotel facilities in Philadelphia were no longer adequate for the Association's meetings, and it was agreed that annual meetings should thenceforth rotate in a regular sequence among Washington, New York, Chicago, Boston, and San Francisco, with the possibility of an occasional meeting being held in Philadelphia if new hotel facilities made it possible. During the 1960s interest was recurringly shown in possible meetings in Miami or Denver or New Orleans; but arguments that such meeting places were inconveniently far from any concentration of Association members and therefore impractical for Association purposes always prevailed.

Growth of Asian Studies throughout the country was reflected during these years of growth also by the emergence of regional meetings of specialists under Association auspices. An informal series of meetings of the New York metropolitan area specialists had begun in the early 1950s, and groups in Upstate New York, in Southern California, and in the Southeastern states soon became organized. In 1960 the Association's Board of Directors adopted a general policy of sanctioning such meetings as regional conferences of the Association and providing them limited financial support. It became the practice for the President of the Association to be the featured

guest speaker at such regional conferences. By
1965 the New York metropolitan area group had become inactive, but new regional conferences had
been organized in New England and in the Rocky
Mountain states. By 1968 the regional conferences had settled into a pattern of six stable
groups: the Midwest Conference on Asian Affairs,
the Western Regional Conference (a combination
of the former Southern California and Rocky Mountain groups), the Southeastern Regional Conference, the New England Regional Conference, the
Upstate New York Regional Conference, and Asian
Studies on the Pacific Coast (first organized in
1966). The Midwest Conference on Asian Affairs
had originated as a separate organization in the
1950s and for a time had published a separate
series of annual papers; its affiliation with
the Association as a regional conference developed only in 1966-67. The regional conferences
all grew out of local initiatives, and in some
cases, notably the Midwest Conference on Asian
Affairs and Asian Studies on the Pacific Coast,
their formation reflected antagonisms toward and
a sense of competition with the national Association. In some of the regional conferences continuity of organization is provided by region-
ally-elected executive groups, but for the most
part responsibility for annual meetings is
merely passed on from one host institution to
another. The regional meetings normally last
one and a half or two days, and their programs
follow the established pattern of the national
annual meeting of the Association. They serve as
a convenient and valuable contact and outlet
primarily for specialists who are not located at
major graduate centers, for whom travel to the
national annual meeting is too expensive, or who
feel overwhelmed by the size of the national
annual meeting. The Directors of the Association,
though at times wary of possible fragmentation
trends that could be fostered by the regional

groups, have on the whole consistently viewed the regional conferences as effective means of serving valid needs of some members and of bringing new members into the national Association. In 1966 the Board approved guidelines to control relations between the regional conferences and the Association, and by 1968 the Association was regularly allocating annual subsidies to the regional conferences totaling about $2,500.

Another dimension of the growth of the Association during the 1956-68 period appears in its proliferation of committees and subcommittees to cope with the developmental problems of special areas or to pursue special projects. Because of the special nature of the research materials used by Asian specialists, it was natural that library problems would be among the first to get special attention in this way. In 1949, at the request of the American Library Association, the Association joined in sponsoring a committee to study library development, appointing Arthur W. Hummel of the Library of Congress, Elizabeth Huff of Berkeley, and Osamu Shimizu of Columbia to serve on it. This Joint Committee on Far Eastern Collections did not survive beyond 1953, largely for want of funding to implement any substantial developmental project. But in 1958, with new sources of financial support becoming available, two new committees were approved: a Committee on American Library Resources on Southern Asia (CALROSA) and a Committee on American Library Resources on the Far East (CALRFE). By 1968 CALROSA, which since 1964 had published a newsletter entitled *South Asian Library and Research Notes*, had been transformed into a South Asia Microform Committee and CALRFE, publishing a *Newsletter* of its own since 1963, had become a Committee on East Asian Libraries. The work of these library committees had been funded by the

Association from its general funds and from its Ford Foundation grants and in part by special grants from the Social Science Research Council and the National Science Foundation.

The biggest library-oriented service project undertaken by the Association began to develop in 1963 under the aegis of CALRFE, primarily because of the entrepreneurial initiative of a Harvard graduate student then studying in Taiwan, Robert L. Irick. It was a time when American collections of Chinese language materials were developing rapidly and in large numbers, and Taiwan book dealers were producing or reprinting works in ever increasing volume to serve this growing market; but there was no effective information and marketing system. With CALRFE encouragement, Irick began to provide American libraries and scholars with information about Chinese books that were available in Taiwan and to serve as a central purchasing agent. At its regular meeting in spring 1964 the Board of Directors allocated an initial subvention of $5,000 to capitalize this venture, acknowledging it as a nonprofit Association activity called the Chinese Materials and Research Aids Service Center (CMRASC). The Center always suffered the handicap of inadequate capitalization despite subsequent infusions of new Association funds from Ford Foundation grants, but the services it provided proved so valuable that its gross annual business grew almost phenomenally to more than $250,000 in 1968. Legal questions about the Association's involvement in such an activity arose from the beginning and gave the Board some uneasiness, and the Directors repeatedly tried to devise ways of "spinning off" CMRASC into a stable independent existence while extricating the Association from direct responsibility for it. To this end, the Service Center was incorporated separately in 1966 as a

wholly-owned subsidiary of the Association.
Since the Service Center needed some continuing
relationship with the Association to maintain
its tax-exempt status and to retain its prestige
in Taiwan, and since it provided services that
were increasingly valued by large numbers of
Association members, no further dissociation
proved feasible. Awkwardness about the operation arose principally from resentment among
some American reprint publishers about the tax-
exempt, Association-subsidized competition of
the Service Center, especially when it began
encouraging and providing a sales outlet for
Taiwan reprints of Western-language works relating to Asian Studies. In 1967-68 negotiations
between concerned American bookmen and officers
of the Association resulted in an understanding
that the Service Center would continue its
distribution of Chinese-language materials un-
hindered and unchallenged, but that it would
restrict its sales of Western-language materials
to individual members of the Association.

The special problems involved in teaching
Asian languages also received particular attention. One of the earliest special-project committees of the Association was a joint committee
with the American Oriental Society to study the
problem of romanizing Chinese. The committee
reported in 1952 that it disliked the Wade-Giles
system of romanization, could not agree on adoption of an alternative system to replace it, and
was opposed to the development of a new system.
The Directors suggested that the committee continue its deliberations, but the committee
gradually became inactive--perhaps in part because of the official adoption of a new romanization system by the Chinese mainland government, which it was assumed might eventually
resolve the issue. But the Association's
interest in language problems by no means
ceased. In 1961 a preexisting Committee on

South Asian Languages, fostered by the American
Council of Learned Societies, was accepted as a
regular project committee of the Association.
It had already conducted a series of studies
and materials-preparation projects under Ford
Foundation auspices, and under Association auspices it provided a continuing forum for
contacts among South Asian language teachers.
In 1963 a newly-formed membership group of
Japanese language teachers was accepted as a
special-interest Committee on the Teaching of
the Japanese Language. Since that year it has
published its own *Journal-Newsletter of the
Association of Teachers of Japanese* three times
a year. In 1966 a comparable membership organization in the Chinese field emerged and began
publication of a thrice-yearly *Journal of the
Chinese Language Teachers Association*. In the
following year the Association of Asian Studies
accepted joint sponsorship, together with the
Modern Language Association, of the Chinese
Language Teachers Association.

Another special interest represented in the
Association from an early time has been the
fostering of Asian studies in secondary education. In 1955 the Board of Directors responded
favorably to a request from the American Council
of Learned Societies that it appoint a Committee
on the Relation of Learned Societies to American
Education (COROLSAE), to work in conjunction
with a committee of the Council and a counter-
part committee of the American Oriental Society
to study and make recommendations about the
proper place and the fostering of Asian Studies
at all levels of American education. Under the
chairmanship of Ronald S. Anderson of Michigan,
long-time Secretary of the Association (1953-56,
1958-60), this committee, though without special
funding, worked to foster supplementary training
of teachers in summer institutes concentrating
on Far Eastern and Asian subjects, and offered

consultative services to the United States Office of Education about the implementation of the National Defense Education Act of 1958. Its principal effectiveness lay in providing information-center services through the Association's Secretariat and in the *Newsletter*. This committee was reorganized as a Committee on Asian Studies in Secondary Education in 1960, but without the personal interest of Anderson after his moving from Michigan to the University of Hawaii it lost vitality and was disbanded in 1963. Meantime a more durable interest among the Association's members had focused on developmental problems in undergraduate education. In 1960 a separately-generated National Committee on Undergraduate Training in Oriental Studies was accepted as a committee of the Association. In 1963 it was restructured as a Committee on Asian Studies in Undergraduate Education. It has served the principal function of providing forums at the annual meeting and at regional conferences for members primarily concerned with undergraduate teaching, and most especially in liberal arts colleges.

Other special-interest committees focused on research conferences and projects. The earliest of these groups to emerge was the Committee on Chinese Thought, which was welcomed under Association sponsorship in 1955 after having been in existence since 1951 with foundation funding and having already sponsored two major research conferences. Under the chairmanship of Arthur F. Wright of Stanford (later of Yale), this committee continued to generate research conferences and published four distinguished symposium volumes before it disbanded itself in 1962. The last four years of the committee's activities were supported by a Rockefeller Foundation grant of $57,400 given the Association in 1957 specifically for this purpose. A group of Japan specialists led by John W. Hall sought comparable recognition by the Association in 1960, becoming a Conference on Modern Japan intending to sponsor similarly-organized research conferences. A grant of $135,000 from the Ford Foundation supported its activities through 1968, including the convening of six conferences and the publication of four distinguished symposium volumes. Then in 1968 the Conference on Modern Japan severed its ties with the Association to become a more broadly concerned Joint Committee on Japanese Studies under sponsorship of the American Council of Learned Societies and the Social Science Research Council. A separate, noncontinuing group of Japan specialists obtained partial support from the Association for a research conference in 1963 that resulted in the publication the following year of a symposium volume entitled *Ministers of Modernization: Elite Mobility in the Meiji Restoration*, which was edited by Bernard S. Silberman of Arizona. A much larger scholarly undertaking came under Association sponsorship in 1960 with the establishment of a Ming Biographical History Project Committee, whose purpose was to organize scholars on an international scale to prepare a biographical Dictionary of important personages in Ming dynasty China. With relatively small-scale financial support from the Association and various other sources, and with substantial funding from the Ford Foundation beginning in 1963, a Ming Project editorial headquarters was established at Columbia University and began publishing a continuing series of *Draft Ming Biographies* fascicles in 1964. The Project Committee, with partial funding from the Association, also participated in sponsoring a research conference on Ming government in 1965 and a research conference on Ming thought in 1966. These conferences resulted in the publication of two symposium volumes of scholarly papers:

Chinese Government in Ming Times: Seven Studies,
edited by Charles O. Hucker of Michigan (1969),
and *Self and Society in Ming Thought*, edited by
W. Theodore de Bary of Columbia (1970).

The Association's Committee on South Asia in
1956 was given an initial three-year support
grant of $10,100 by the Rockefeller Foundation,
which enabled it to sponsor a number of meetings
of South Asian specialists for organizational
purposes. It also sponsored separately-funded
surveys resulting in the publication of two useful reference volumes: *Resources for South Asian
Language Studies in the United States,* edited by
W. Norman Brown of Pennsylvania (1961), and
*Resources for South Asian Area Studies in the
United States,* edited by Richard D. Lambert of
Pennsylvania (1962). The Committee on South
Asia also fostered the development of more
specialized committees, which in effect became
its subcommittees. These included a Tagore
Memorial Lectureship Committee, which existed
from 1961 to 1968 to sponsor a series of
outside-funded lectures, four volumes of which
had been published by 1968. A Committee on
State Politics in India, with outside funding,
sponsored a research conference that led to
publication of a symposium volume entitled *State
Politics in India,* edited by Myron Weiner, in
1967. Other subcommittees that emerged were a
Ceylon Studies Committee, a Bengal Studies Committee, a Gandhi Centennial Committee, and a
Ghalib Centenary Committee; all of these quickly
became involved in sponsoring conferences, lectures, and publications. In 1967 the parent
Committee on South Asia jointly sponsored a
special research conference on the untouchables
in contemporary India, out of which a symposium
volume was planned.

In the pattern of the South Asian organization, a Committee on Southeast Asia came into
being in 1962. With Asia Society funding, it

promptly sponsored a conference which produced
a volume published in 1963 under the title
Southeast Asia: Problems of U.S. Policy, edited
by William Henderson. It also sponsored the
creation of an auxiliary agency, the Inter-
University Planning Committee on Southeast Asian
Studies, which had an organizational meeting
early in 1968. A subcommittee on archives and
documents relating to Southeast Asia had begun
planning an international conference about micro-
filming important documentary materials.

Among the other activities of these sorts
that were sponsored by the Association between
1956 and 1968 was the "U Nu Honorary Lectureship," which brought distinguished Burmans for
lecture tours of American colleges during the
three years beginning in 1957, under a $25,000
grant from the Asia Foundation.

Most of the special-interest or developmental
activities mentioned above originated among
small groups of interested members. The policy
generally followed by the Board of Directors
was to invite and foster such initiatives from
outside the leadership, but the Board itself
took the initiative in several instances. Among
these was the creation in 1961 of an International Liaison Committee, which ever since has
recurringly made special efforts to bring distinguished foreign scholars to the Association's
annual meetings and to help American scholars
establish and maintain contacts with foreign
counterparts whenever possible. Also, the Board
for several years tried to develop interest in
the creation of a special body to promote
Korean studies and finally in 1967 achieved this
purpose with the establishment of a Korean
Studies Committee. It was in considerable degree in response to encouragement from the Board
and the Secretariat that a Buddhist Studies
Committee came to be established in 1967. On a
larger scale, the Board committed the

Association to join the American Oriental Society in seeking to bring the triennial meeting of the International Congress of Orientalists to the United States in 1964 and, failing in that, successfully brought the 1967 meeting to the United States; it was held at Ann Arbor, under sponsorship of the University of Michigan. The Association's Secretariat undertook the enormously time-consuming task of serving as administrative agency for the Congress to assist Russell H. Fifield, former Secretary of the Association, in carrying out his functions as Secretary-General of the 1967 Congress.

The proliferating activities of the Association and its committees from 1956 into 1968, and the greatly expanded financial aspects of Association management that followed, put great strains on the organizational apparatus. To cope with its new level of responsibilities, the Board of Directors met twice a year from 1961 through 1964, once in the fall as well as in conjunction with the annual membership meeting in the spring. This practice was abandoned in the end for the sake of economy; after 1964 a large proportion of Board decision-making business had to be carried on in the form of irregularly-mailed information circulars and ballots issuing from the Secretary. Previously, in 1958, an Executive Committee consisting of the President, Vice-President, Secretary, Treasurer, Editor of the *Journal*, and Editor of the Monograph Series had initiated the regular practice of meeting in advance of the Board meeting to try to organize Association business in such a way that the Board could manage its agenda most efficiently. In other steps to maintain control over the increasingly complex business of the Association, the Board in 1957 authorized creation of a Finance Committee to oversee the work of the Treasurer and to advise him about investments, and in 1958 created an

Advisory Committee on Research and Development.
Its members were appointed on a long-term,
rotational basis, and its mandate was "to con-
duct a continuing survey and appraisal of needs
and activities in the field of Asian studies,
to advise the officers and Directors of the
Association for Asian Studies on developmental
activities and relations with foundations and
other outside organizations, and to maintain
contact with the committees" of the Association.

At its regular spring meeting in 1961, the
Board of Directors confronted the administrative
problem of coping with its greatly expanded
business and appointed two ad hoc committees to
recommend more effective ways of proceeding: a
committee on publications under the chairmanship
of Charles O. Hucker, then of Arizona, and a
committee on reorganization under the chairmanship of Robert Scalapino of Berkeley. These ad
hoc committees coordinated their efforts and
submitted recommendations to the Board in the
fall of 1961. At that time the Board approved a
series of steps intended to simplify and clarify
administration of the Association: (1) Consoli-
dating the *Newsletter of the Committee on South
Asia* into one unified *Newsletter of the Association for Asian Studies* and publishing it in
substantial pamphlet format; (2) Making the
Bibliography of Asian Studies editorially independent of the *Journal,* though continuing to
publish it as a fifth issue of the *Journal;* (3)
Allowing for a broadened scope of Association
publications by changing the Monograph Series
into a series newly called Monographs and Papers
of the Association; (4) Establishing a Publications Committee comprising the Editors of the
Journal, the *Bibliography,* and the Monographs
and Papers and chaired by a current member of
the Board; (5) Providing for greater continuity
in the executive leadership of the Association
by establishing the office of Second Vice-

President, who would normally be expected to succeed to the Vice-Presidency and then to the Presidency; (6) Formally constituting a Finance Committee comprising the Secretary, the Treasurer, one or more members appointed by the Board, and the Vice-President serving as chairman; and (7) Formally constituting an Executive Committee comprising the President, the First and Second Vice-Presidents, the Secretary, the Treasurer, the Chairman of the Publications Committee, and the Chairman of the Advisory Committee on Research and Development. Appropriate amendments in the Constitution and By-laws were adopted by mail ballot of the membership in 1962.

In 1963, when the Association's general funds had attained stability at a high level, a change in investment policy was authorized by the Board. On the advice of the new Finance Committee, Association funds were taken out of savings and loan associations, and it was approved that they be invested in bonds and stocks under the supervision of the Finance Committee. In 1967, taking note of continuing inflationary trends in the national economy, the Board authorized an aggressive investment policy to maximize income for the Association's general fund equity.

During the long period of steady and substantial growth and expansion from 1956 to 1968, the Board of Directors did turn its back on one possibility for even greater growth, an opportunity to include Middle Eastern specialists whose interests were not satisfactorily met by existing learned societies. At its spring meeting in 1962 the Board welcomed William Schorger of Michigan as a spokesman for such Middle Eastern specialists, who were then attempting to organize themselves under joint sponsorship of the American Council of Learned Societies and the Social Science Research

Council. They were considering three alternatives: (1) affiliation with the American Oriental Society, (2) affiliation with the Association for Asian Studies, and (3) establishment of an independent society. An informal poll of the Association's officers and directors revealed widely varying attitudes: six were in favor of including the Middle Eastern group, six were against doing so, and seven were neutral. The matter was consequently referred to the Advisory Committee on Research and Development for further study. When the Board next met in the autumn of 1962, after hearing recommendations from the Advisory Committee, it agreed to offer a kind of "fraternal assistance" to the Middle Eastern specialists for a period of three years to facilitate their creating their own society and obtaining initial foundation support; but the Board would not approve absorbing the Middle East group into the Association in the fashion of its previous absorption of South Asian specialists. The Middle East group, apparently considering the Association's attitude inauspicious, never took advantage of the "fraternal assistance" that was offered and went about establishing their own society through other channels.

Not long before, in 1960, the Association had lost what seemed like a good possibility of further expansion when a group of scholars, almost all of whom were members of the Association, formed themselves into a Committee on Contemporary China. The new Committee voted to seek sponsorship of the Association, but in the end, "after a small minority overrode this decision" (it was reported to the Association), it sought and obtained status as a joint committee under the aegis of the American Council of Learned Societies and the Social Science Research Council. Particularly since it soon attracted substantial foundation funding for a variety of

scholarly projects, the Board of Directors for
several meetings thereafter expressed distress
and regret about what had happened.

The rapid growth of the Association between
1956 and 1968 can be attributed to a number of
things, including in some measure activities of
the Association itself--the growing reputation
and influence of its publications, the careful
preparation of annual meetings by successive
Program Committees, the fluctuating vigor of its
successive Membership Committees, and in general
the variety of services it offered its membership. But the Association's growth naturally
reflected a corresponding or even greater growth
of the clientele, the enormously increasing
numbers of American teachers, students, and
institutions seriously concerned with Asian
Studies. This growth of the profession was in
part the cumulative result of extensive pump-
priming efforts on the part of the American
Council of Learned Societies, the Social Science
Research Council, the Rockefeller Foundation,
the Carnegie Corporation, the Ford Foundation,
the Asia Society, the Japan Society, the China
Society, the Asia Foundation, and similar
bodies including some colleges and universities
that vigorously promoted the field. It was
affected by American involvement in the Korean
War beginning in 1950 and in the civil war that
developed in Vietnam after the dissolution of
French Indo-China in 1956, which gave new gen-
erations of American youths first-hand
experience in Asia and kept the attention of the
American government and public focused on Asia.
It was affected too by continuing American concern about and interest in the rapid and
obviously important political and social
changes that were occurring in all parts of
Asia throughout the 1950s and 1960s. Most of
all, probably, growth of the profession was
facilitated by Congressional approval of the

National Defense Education Act (NDEA) of 1958, which authorized a steady flow of millions of dollars of federal funds into fellowships, instructional programs, library expansion, summer institutes and workshops, and research projects relating to language and area studies of the less well studied regions of the world, particularly Asia. Although the Association never received direct general support from the federal government under the NDEA program, it benefited indirectly in countless ways from NDEA stimulation of professional development in the field.

Through all these years of rapid expansion the Association's Secretariat remained a relatively small operation in Ann Arbor, in quarters provided by The University of Michigan. Although there had been recurring talk about the possible need for a professional Executive Secretary since the formation of the Association, successive Secretaries drawn from The University of Michigan faculty continued to serve the Association without compensation and without being released from any of their normal academic duties at the university. Under their "after-hours" supervision, so to speak, the office was run by the Association's extraordinarily dedicated Manager with the assistance of one full-time assistant. The office staff was expanded temporarily to serve the needs of the 1967 International Congress of Orientalists, but by 1968, as life in the Secretariat returned more or less to normal, it became increasingly apparent that in its current staffing position it could not adequately cope with the business of the Association. For that matter, it was apparent that the Association had reached an important new turning point in its over-all development.

ACCUMULATING PROBLEMS OF THE ASSOCIATION'S
ROLE AND ORGANIZATION

In 1967-68, following so long a period of growth
and expansion, the Association's Board of Directors undertook a thorough reevaluation of the
Association's organization, functions, and
services. The kinds of questions that arose can
be discussed in three categories: (1) questions
about the Association's relations with its
members, (2) questions about the leadership
structure of the Association, and (3) questions
about the proper mission of the Association.

The Association's Relations
with Its Members

During the 1960s the Association for Asian
Studies came to be widely known among American
learned societies as one having an extraordinarily high level of member participation. A 1968
questionnaire responded to by approximately one
quarter of its entire membership suggested that
the respondents were on the whole satisfied
with the functioning of the Association and
with the services it provided them. By a ratio
of 308 to 180 they reported that they attended
annual meetings of the Association more often
than the annual meetings of their respective
discipline-oriented societies. At the same time,

45

the respondents reflected discontent with various aspects of the Association, of which the leadership had not been wholly unaware. All members no doubt regretted the inevitable depersonalization of the Association as it increased in size and the concomitant bureaucratization of its operations. There were also more specific discontents and tensions.

Many of the tensions--and much of the vitality--of the Association derive from the heterogeneous nature of its membership. At the time of its origin as a membership organization in 1948, some members felt that the Association should maintain an elitist quality by accepting into membership only persons with specialized scholarly interests in the field, but the predominant view by far was that all persons who wished to become members should be welcomed. The 1955-56 inclusion of South Asia within the Association's sphere of interest increased diversity within the membership, as did the Association's original, unchallenged, and continuing commitment to encompass both premodern and contemporary and both humanistic and social scientific interests. The membership therefore includes internationally recognized scholars as well as students who are virtual beginners in the field and many nonacademic persons including government employees, businessmen, and churchmen. Among the Association's academic members (by far the largest group) are professors and students at major graduate centers who are totally absorbed in advanced and specialized teaching and scholarship; professors at other institutions who, while doing specialized research on one area or period, teach broader courses on East Asia or South Asia or perhaps all of Asia and may teach still other courses not relating to Asia; and professors, students, and secondary teachers who, while not considering themselves scholarly specialists in any aspect of Asian studies, regularly incorporate Asian subject matter in their studying and teaching. In 1968 there were 404 foreign members resident in 40 different countries, Canada and Japan leading the list by far. The 3,318 domestic members were spread unevenly throughout the United States, with heaviest concentrations along the East Coast from Boston to Washington, in California, and in the Great Lakes states, and with lightest scatterings in the central South and in the western mountain areas. Academic members represented almost all conceivable disciplines but historians and political scientists were predominant. In terms of area of interest, China specialists were the largest single group; Southeast Asian and South Asian specialists each constituted 12 or 13 percent of the membership. If one combined the names of all those specializing in East Asia (China, Korea, Japan), they made up well over half of the membership.

Inevitably, as the Association's varied membership grew toward a total of 5,000 and participants in its annual meetings grew toward a total of 2,000, it became increasingly easy for many individual members to feel that their views and interests were not appropriately represented or served. The Board fostered and encouraged both a great variety of special-interest committees and a group of regional conferences serving every area of the United States, in part to provide activities in which large numbers of members could participate and with which they could in some measure identify. Successive Program Committees and successive Editors of the *Journal*, sometimes under prodding from the Board of Directors, tried to maximize membership interest by providing topical or problem-oriented program sessions that combined premodern with modern material or that cut across Asia's regional segments, and *Journal* articles or groups of articles that had all-Asia relevance, while at the same time trying to maintain appropriate outlets for more narrowly specialized papers and articles that were wanted by many members.

Inter-group tensions and rivalries nevertheless persisted in the membership. Some East Asian specialists after 1955-56, when South Asia was added to the geographic sphere of the Association, felt that the Association had lost its original quality as a kind of small club in which everyone knew everyone; for them, it had become too large, too diversified, and too impersonal. Although other considerations were of some importance (for example, a feeling that the Middle East had little cultural relevance to either South or East Asia), it was principally the vigorous and sometimes emotional opposition to further diversification on the part of such East Asian specialists that accounted for the Association's rather cool reaction to tentative overtures from Middle Eastern specialists in 1962. South Asian and Southeast Asian specialists seem on the whole to have been much more amenable to the possible inclusion of the Middle Eastern group in the Association.

Similar tensions and differences have existed in the Association between members associated with large and prestigious graduate centers and, on the other hand, those associated with smaller and less prestigious programs or isolated in institutions without substantial development of Asian Studies in the whole curriculum. Mixed up with these tensions are natural differences of interests between senior and junior scholars, between established teacher-scholars and their students, and between native Asians in the profession and non-Asians. Institutional rivalries also appear among those members associated with major centers. Most widespread has been a "grassroots" feeling that the Association is dominated too much by an "Establishment" comprising the large Ivy League schools together with Michigan, Chicago, Berkeley, Stanford, and Washington. Occasional "anti-Establishment" feelings have appeared in the Association's elections, as in 1967 when Shunzo Sakamaki of the University of Hawaii, having been nominated by petition and elected to the Board of Directors in 1964, was nominated by petition for the second vice presidency. Although he was not elected, his nomination and his showing in the balloting gave evidence that a substantial number of members were not happy with the Association's traditional electoral patterns.

The 1968 questionnaire returns showed that the membership was not fully satisfied with the services then provided by the Association. Many respondents gave high priorities to more active promotion of Asian studies in secondary education, more vigorous efforts to provide information about dissertations completed and in progress and about scholarly activities outside the United States, and more active job registry and placement services.

Problems of Leadership in the Association

As has been intimated above, by 1968 some members believed that the Association was run by an "elitist oligarchy" principally from "eastern in-group" schools. Perhaps the same criticism can be made of every national learned society in the United States. Certainly, in this regard the Association was clearly vulnerable to criticism. Of the first twenty Presidents, thirteen were faculty members at Ivy League universities: Rupert Emerson, Edwin O. Reischauer, and John K. Fairbank of Harvard (Charles S. Gardner not included, though a resident of Cambridge and long associated with Harvard); L. Carrington Goodrich and Hugh Borton

of Columbia; Kenneth S. Latourette, Arthur F.
Wright, Karl J. Pelzer, and John W. Hall of
Yale; Lauriston Sharp and Knight Biggerstaff of
Cornell; William W. Lockwood of Princeton; and
W. Norman Brown of Pennsylvania. George B.
Cressey of Syracuse and Arthur W. Hummel of the
Library of Congress would also generally be con-
sidered members of the "eastern in-group,"
though not associated with major graduate
centers of Asian Studies. Earl H. Pritchard of
Chicago, Felix M. Keesing of Stanford, and
Robert B. Hall of Michigan, though not "east-
erners," represented large graduate centers.
The 1950-51 President, Harold S. Quigley of
Minnesota, was the only President of the Asso-
ciation who was associated neither with the East
nor with a major graduate center of Asian
Studies. Predominance of the "eastern in-group"
was perpetuated when nominations and elections
assured the succession to the presidency of
Holden Furber of Pennsylvania in 1968, W.
Theodore de Bary of Columbia in 1969, Cora
DuBois of Harvard in 1970, and C. Martin Wilbur
of Columbia in 1971.

Probably no member of the Association would
have argued that these successive Presidents
were undistinguished. The distinction of the
Presidents is evidenced by the fact that, for
example, Latourette and Fairbank also were
chosen presidents of the American Historical Association, Goodrich and Brown also were chosen
presidents of the American Oriental Society, and
Cressey also served as president of the International Geographical Union and honorary president
of the Association of American Geographers. But
it was resented by many members that such important centers of Asian Studies as Berkeley and
Washington and (in recent years) Hawaii never
gained representation in the presidency; that
areas of the United States outside the East
Coast were very poorly represented; and that no

scholar of Asian extraction had ever been elected President.

Defining the leadership of the Association from 1948 through 1969 more broadly, to include all elected Directors and appointed Secretaries and Treasurers in addition to the Presidents, produces a somewhat different picture. Areas other than the central and northern East Coast were better represented, and institutions that were not thought of as major graduate centers of Asian Studies were also represented: Brooklyn, Bryn Mawr, Colgate, Dartmouth, Duke, Haverford, Johns Hopkins, Minnesota (but by no one except Quigley), Massachusetts Institute of Technology, Northwestern, New York University, Ohio University, Oberlin, Arizona, Florida, University of California at Los Angeles, and Wisconsin. But the leadership in this broader definition was still dominated by what some might call an "elitist oligarchy." Michigan, in part by being the long-time base of the Secretariat, was represented 18 times in this leadership, Harvard 12 times, Columbia 10 times, Yale and Berkeley 9 times, Chicago 7 times, Cornell 6 times, Pennsylvania 5 times, Syracuse 4 times; and Washington, Princeton, and Stanford 3 times each. Defining the leadership even more broadly to include other appointive positions that are important in decision-making procedures of the Association—the various Editors, the Chairman of the Nominating Committee, the Chairman of the Advisory Committee on Research and Development, and the Chairman of the powerful Committee on South Asia —merely confirms the trends so clear in other analyses.

In sum, it would seem fair to say that during the history of the Association to date, and particularly through 1968, its affairs were dominated by members from major graduate centers, especially those of the central and northern East Coast area, and most particularly those of the Ivy League. The history of the Association in this regard had not fulfilled either the expressed intention of the Board of Directors when it established the early policy that the presidency should "alternate between the different regions of the U.S. as much as circumstances will permit," or the Constitutional prescriptions about representation on the Board. There are, of course, understandable explanations for this. The names of scholars at major graduate centers are better known throughout the membership than others. The programs along the north and central East Coast are generally older and more solidly established than those elsewhere; their prestige, their library facilities, and sometimes their higher salary scales have enabled them to attract both promising younger scholars and outstanding older ones from other programs. Berkeley and Chicago have had comparable advantages, but many of their Asian specialists (as in the case of Pennsylvania) have chosen to maintain closer ties with the American Oriental Society than with the Association--e.g., Yuen Ren Chao and Peter Boodberg of Berkeley and Herrlee G. Creel of Chicago, who have been elected to the presidency of the Society but have chosen not to play prominent roles in the affairs of the Association. In any event, predominance of the "eastern in-group" in the leadership of the Association, defensible as it may be, has been resented as Asian Studies programs have spread more widely throughout the country.

The Board of Directors at an early time also established a policy that the presidency should "alternate as much as possible on the one hand between scholars representing the humanities and the social sciences and on the other between scholars primarily interested in" the different regions of Asia; and By-laws of the Association have consistently enjoined that nominations for the Board should be made in an attempt to achieve balanced representation along these lines. On the whole, the history of the Association shows a somewhat better record in this regard. But imbalances have occurred, and some have persisted. Historians and social scientists have almost always had still greater representation in the leadership than their predominant representation in the membership, whereas humanists have almost never attained representation in the leadership approaching their representation in the membership. Japan specialists have been significantly overrepresented in the leadership in proportion to their representation in the membership, but their leadership role has been declining in recent years; China specialists have consistently been overrepresented in the leadership to a lesser extent, and their overrepresentation shows few signs of declining; South Asia specialists have on balance played a role in the leadership equivalent to their representation in the membership, but they have been significantly overrepresented in the leadership in recent years; and Southeast Asia specialists have rather consistently been underrepresented in the leadership in proportion to their representation in the membership. The humanists in the Japan field have no doubt been the one substantial group in the membership that has consistently been underrepresented in the leadership.

Again, understandable factors account in some part for these imbalances in the leadership. By their nature, humanists are perhaps less likely to seek leadership roles than are historians and social scientists and less likely to find gratification in organizational connections. They are perhaps more likely to have a broader range of outlets for their publications and presentations than their historian and social-science counterparts in the Association. Because of recent political history, China specialists perhaps feel a greater need to obtain strong organizational support than, for example, Japan specialists do. As has already been indicated, South Asian specialists have been aware of antagonism toward them on the part of some members of the original Far Eastern Association and have perhaps asserted themselves within the Association more aggressively than, for example, Japan and Southeast Asian specialists have felt a need to do.

All imbalances in the leadership of the Association result, of course, from a combination of factors including appointments and policy decisions made by the Board, nominations submitted by the Nominating Committee, and electoral peculiarities on the part of the membership. For fear that many worthy candidates for the presidency would not accept nomination on a competitive slate, successive Boards of Directors consistently resisted multiple nominations for the presidential and vice-presidential positions. Respondents to a questionnaire distributed among the membership in 1967–68 showed a strong preference, 413 to 268, for multiple nominations, and the Board in 1968 authorized the Nominating Committee to submit multiple nominations for the second vice-presidency for 1969 balloting. But the Nominating Committee chose not to do so. In the case of balloting for vacancies on the Board of Directors, the policy has always been to nominate more members than can be elected: the common practice has been for the Nominating Committee to propose the names of twice as many nominees as there are vacancies. Groups of members have always been able to put names on the ballot by petition, and the Nominating Committee has been authorized to identify on the ballot those persons who are nominated by petition. "Anti-establishment" feelings among the membership have always been considered the explanation for the fact that almost every nominee-by-petition for the Board has been elected. All these procedures and practices ensure that the Nominating Committee cannot actually manipulate the preparation of the ballot so as to dictate the composition of the Board of Directors. They also prevent the Nominating Committee from ensuring, by its pattern of nominations, that existing imbalances in the composition of the Board at any time will be rectified.

The Nominating Committee plays an important and delicate role in the affairs of the Association, and it has recurringly taken abuse, deserved or undeserved, for strange electoral situations that have offended some members. There was discontent that Columbia University men should be successive presidents in 1956-57 and 1957-58, and that a "Yale dynasty" should occupy the presidency three years out of four, from 1964 to 1968. In 1957 the Nominating Committee placed one of its own members on the ballot in such a combination of nominees that, as the sole Southeast Asian specialist on the ballot, his election was assured. The consequence of this was unanimous adoption by the Board in 1958 of the policy that "individuals serving on the Nominating Committee should not during their term of office accept nomination even by petition to any elective office within the Association." Distress about the Nominating Committee was also expressed in 1963, when no South Asian specialists were nominated for the Board; in 1965, when three Southeast Asian specialists were nominated for the Board with the result that ballots were divided among them and none was elected; and in 1968, when three University of Chicago men appeared on the ballot as nominees for the Board.

In 1959 the Board of Directors established a vague policy that, whereas members of the Program Committee "should have youth and energy," the Nominating Committee should be constituted of members who could be relied on to be "responsible and mature." In general, successive Nominating Committees seem to have made conscientious efforts to provide a flow of qualified people for the elective offices, but they failed conspicuously to ensure that the leadership of the Association proportionately represented the area interests, the disciplinary interests, and the regional distribution throughout the United States of the membership. Their failures were by no means all due to any lack of "responsible and mature" efforts; in considerable part, their failures were a measure of the impossibility of satisfying all the divergent demands made on them.

Members who had no experience in positions of leadership in the Association found it easy at all times to conceive of the leadership as a monolithic, oligarchic establishment. Within the leadership group, however, there have always been divisive forces at work. Directors have sometimes felt that the President or the Secretary was running the Association without paying more than lip-service to the authority of the Board. In 1968 it was even suggested that the Directors should have their own Chairman of the Board, as a check on the authority of the President. Presidents and Directors alike have often felt they were bypassed or manipulated by an aggressive Secretary.

The most notable instance of divisiveness within the leadership was a controversy about the role of the Advisory Committee on Research and Development (ACRD) that spanned the years 1958-1961. The forerunner of this committee had been established in 1955 for the purpose of negotiating with the Ford Foundation for the Association's first general-support Ford grant, and in 1956 it was disbanded when that grant had been awarded. Its existence reflected the view that an elected group such as the Directors could not necessarily be the experienced, responsible, high-prestige group that an outside agency such as a foundation would confidently deal with. A similar view shaped ACRD when it was established in 1958 under the chairmanship of Fairbank of Harvard. That is, there was a feeling, seldom openly expressed in quite such blunt terms, that the Board of Directors, as elected representatives of an open-membership body, was not necessarily the wisest judge of how the Association's funds and efforts should be expended in fostering the profession's scholarly development. ACRD was intended to be a group of senior, experienced scholars appointed on a long-term basis, but in a rotational pattern, to give careful consideration to the quality of funding proposals and developmental proposals and to make recommendations to the Board, since the latter, because of the pressure of routine administrative business, could not be a study group. Directors were naturally jealous of their powers, and ACRD was repeatedly reviewed by the Board in discussions intimating that ACRD threatened to usurp functions that properly belonged to the Board alone. At one point serious consideration was given to the abolition of ACRD, on the grounds that it tended to meddle in the administrative affairs of the Association. The opposing view was that ACRD needed a continuing overview of all Association affairs in order to play its advisory role properly. In 1961, after the matter had been discussed annually, an ACRD policy proposal was accepted by the Board, to the effect that:

1. The function of ACRD is advisory to the Board of Directors.
2. The ACRD will give to the Board advice on:
   a. Such matters as are referred to it

by the Board through the President
or Secretary acting for the President;

    b. Such matters as the ACRD, itself,
may feel should be considered by
the Board in the interests of the
advancement of Asian Studies.

This apparent resolution of the controversy,
authorizing ACRD to act on its own initiative,
was reversed when the Association was generally
reorganized in 1962. The new Constitution and
By-laws adopted in that year prescribed that ACRD
"shall carry out investigations and make recommendations to the Board of Directors on matters
referred to it by the Chairman of the Board"
(i.e., the President), thus discouraging ACRD
from making recommendations on its own initiative.

    Who, or what group, is the dominant force in
the Association's leadership at any time depends
very largely, of course, on the personalities
involved. The current and immediate past Secretaries are in agreement in judging that the
presidency and the secretaryship, in that order,
are the most influential positions as regards
decision-making within the Association.

Problems about the Mission
of the Association

    As stated in the original Constitution and
By-laws and essentially reiterated in all revisions, the Association's mission is to foster
interest in and promote the scholarly study of
Asia, as a nonprofit and nonpolitical professional organization. Until quite recent years
this concept of its mission has never been challenged, but questions have occasionally been
raised about its interpretation.

    Until recently no one seriously proposed that

58

the Association should engage in extensive
public-education activities. Moreover, there
have always been recurring questions in members'
minds about the extent to which the Association
should concern itself with education at all, as
distinct from scholarship. For the most part,
the Association's leadership has always tended
to consider that teaching should be left to the
institutions concerned, whether they be universities, colleges, secondary schools, or primary
schools. In short, there has been no urge within the Association to assert itself as an
accreditation agency; if anything, such a
notion has been repellent. Most individual members, however, have been active teachers at some
level, and the Association has not wholly dis-
sociated itself from their concerns as teachers.
From 1956 to 1963 the Association sponsored
committees that were primarily concerned with
introducing and fostering Asian Studies in
secondary education; but this interest never
evolved into a major concern of the Association
and by the late 1960s had become dormant. A
goodwill gesture, in response to a request from
the Asia Society, was the authorization in 1964
of a special $2.50 subscription rate to the
Newsletter for secondary-level teachers. Part
of the interest in secondary education had
always focused on the provision of special summer institutes for secondary-teacher training in
Asian Studies. This interest had been expressed
in the earliest years of the Association's existence, and it had its greatest flowering in
the period 1957-1960. To the extent that such
summer institutes expanded into the realm of
training college teachers, the Association at
times expressed some alarm, being concerned lest
inadequately-prepared professors fill college
curriculums with courses that ought to be taught
by Asian Studies specialists. But the Association increasingly recognized that it had an

inescapable special responsibility for encouraging Asian Studies teachers at the undergraduate level and since 1960 has sponsored committees giving them a special organizational focus within the Association. The regional conferences of the Association quite consciously try to serve the special interests of undergraduate teachers and even of secondary-education teachers, although this is by no means their whole function. Nevertheless, it would seem fair to say that the Association has generally chosen not to concern itself vigorously with either secondary or undergraduate education in Asian Studies. Its principal focus of interest has been on scholarship rather than education, and it has avoided involving itself in any direct fashion even with problems of graduate education.

Questions have recurringly arisen about how aggressively the Association should try to provide leadership for Asian Studies development. For the most part, the Association has concentrated rather narrowly on fostering and perpetuating its own particular activities and services and has left developmental initiatives to small groups of its members, to institutions or groups of institutions, to such agencies as the American Council of Learned Societies and the Social Science Research Council, and to foundations. The Association as such played no part, for example, in influencing Congressional action that led to the National Defense Education Act of 1958. Its Secretariat and an ACRD committee did, after NDEA was passed, offer advice and counsel to the Office of Education concerning its implementation, but not very aggressively and without much influence. In 1961 the Board of Directors specifically declined to undertake helping the Office of Education evaluate the implementation of NDEA to that time, when the Office of Education asked the American Council of Learned Societies for guidance in this regard and the Council in turn asked the Association to participate. The same attitude was evident in 1967, when the Board of Directors felt it necessary to "remind" the Committee on Southeast Asia "that projects using government funds must be administered by an institution other than this Association." That most members approved the traditional developmental policy of the Association was clearly indicated by respondents to a questionnaire distributed in 1967-68. In considering possible new functions for the Association, while giving a very high priority to "promotion of Asian studies in secondary education" (interpreted to mean that this was highly desirable in principle, at least), the respondents gave lowest priority to "public information and public education activities."

The Association's unaggressive developmental posture unquestionably derived from the Association's traditional commitment to a nonpolitical role. Its habit has been to shrink from anything that might become a political entanglement, and the reasons for this can be traced clearly in its early history, especially its involvement in the political troubles experienced by the Institute of Pacific Relations.

When the Far Eastern Association was formed in early 1948 the American government was trying to disengage itself from the civil war then raging in China, and the American Institute of Pacific Relations was already under attack by friends of the Chinese Nationalists for allegedly undermining the confidence of the American government and people in the Nationalist government. One of the most prominent challengers of the Institute was Alfred Kohlberg of New York City. Mr. Kohlberg attended the organizational meeting of the Association on April 2, 1948, and reportedly asked pointed questions implying "that the FEA was formed by the IPR for devious reasons." Then on April 30 he wrote a letter to the Trustees of the American Institute of Pacific Relations and the Directors of the Far Eastern Association containing the following statements:

I have heard rumors that the idea of forming this rival institution in the study of Far Eastern affairs originated in the IPR and that its purpose is to have in readiness a new organization of unblemished record to carry on in case the feared indictments of certain IPR officials by the June (1947) Federal Grand Jury were found, or in case of an unpleasant investigation by the American (Un-American?) Activities Committee. . . . In view of these, possibly unfounded, explanations, I thought you might wish to issue a statement explaining why the IPR approves a rival in its field at a time when it professes that funds available from the public and from the Rockefeller, Russell Sage, Columbia and Carnegie Foundations are insufficient for its needs.

These allegations, that the Association was created as a convenient "front" behind which leaders of the embattled Institute of Pacific Relations could seek refuge, have haunted the Association ever since. They were perpetuated in 1951-52, when an extensive public investigation of the Institute of Pacific Relations was conducted by the Internal Security Subcommittee of the Judiciary Committee of the U.S. Senate, principally in testimony given by David Nelson Rowe of Yale, himself a member of the Association until 1961. Pertinent parts of Rowe's testimony include the following statements:

There was a period when the people in the Institute of Pacific Relations were rather alarmed by the tendencies that they saw

62

arising in Government regarding themselves
as an organization. . . . And the problem
of what to do if this thing went on further and the Institute of Pacific Relations itself was put on, say, a list by
the Attorney General, for example, and
named as a front organization, alarmed
these people at least enough so that they
decided they would have to set up some
kind of organization to hold the bag for
them in case this happened. . . . Where
this matter of forming a new organization
was brought up, this was what later became
the Far Eastern Association, and the question specifically discussed was the question of how this organization should be
differentiated from the Institute of
Pacific Relations. . . . There was growing
dissatisfaction with the Institute of
Pacific Relations because of the very
large part it was playing on controversial
issues and the part that it took in talking about policy, instead of acting as a
straight scholarly organization with the
interest of promoting research and study,
serving the interests of the scholarly
fraternity, by affording them publication
media, meetings at which they could read
their papers, and all the activities of a
learned society. . . . At the beginning
you had a very strong interlocking directorate, so to speak, between these two
concerns (i.e., IPR and FEA). And a lot
of the people that you run across in
your study of the Institute of Pacific
Relations are involved on the control
directorate of this association. This is
February 1951.

The connection and the duplication of
personnel, this interlocking directorate
I talk about, is not as close now as it

was at the original formation. . . . Mr. Holland, for example, was represented on the advisory editorial board, I believe. And on an organization of the Far Eastern Association, which I think has since gone out of existence, which was the committee on research work. They now have a monograph series, and they have as editor of the monograph series Mr. Dirk (sic) Bodde, professor at the University of Pennsylvania, a very strong supporter of the Institute of Pacific Relations. He supports it all the time in the public press. Mr. Biggerstaff, who was and probably is on the IPR trustees, was secretary in 1950. John K. Fairbank was at that time vice president. Wilma Fairbank was at that time news editor of the quarterly.

Let's see if there are any other of these names. William L. Holland was a member of the board of directors in November 1950. Owen Lattimore was a member of the board of directors in 1950. George E. Taylor was a member of the board of directors in 1950.

Now, there is a great amount of duplication still at this point.

It may be said, of course, that the number of far eastern specialists in the United States is not very large, and the claim could easily be made that these are the most eminent people in the field. But I would say that as far as general political views are concerned, all those people I named probably share about a 90 percent consensus. And that is the thing I am talking about. They agree with each other on current questions of far eastern politics very strongly.

As late as 1957, in a public press release,

Kohlberg referred to the Association as "the IPR underground thing," and similar allegations were heard in Congress even in 1966.

That there was indeed a kind of "overlapping directorate" between the Institute of Pacific Relations and the Association was easily demonstrated. William L. Holland, Executive Secretary of the International Institute and Executive Vice-President of the American Institute, was a founding member of the Association as a membership organization and served as an elected Director from 1949 to 1950. Owen Lattimore, long-time editor of the Institute's most influential publication, *Pacific Affairs*, served as an elected Director of the Association from 1949 to 1952. Virginia Thompson (who became Mrs. Richard Adloff in the late 1940s), was a staff member of the Institute when she was elected one of the first Directors of the Association in 1948; in 1949 she was elected Vice-President; she served as Chairman of the Nominating Committee in 1951-52; and she and her husband made contributions to the Association that made possible inauguration of the Monograph Series. Many other prominent members of the Association in its early years were also associated with the Institute. As late as 1953 the Board of Trustees of the American Institute included Knight Biggerstaff, Hugh Borton, George B. Cressey, Sidney D. Gamble, L. Carrington Goodrich, and Kenneth S. Latourette, all of whom were active members of the Association; only two Trustees in academic posts were not. In the course of the Congressional hearings on the Institute that were held in 1951-52, 186 current members of the Association (contrasted against 727 total members as of March, 1951) were at least mentioned, in one connection or another.

As Rowe's testimony suggests, this "overlapping directorate" resulted from the fact that prominent Far Eastern specialists in the United

States happened overwhelmingly to have been associated in some fashion with both the Institute and the Association. In retrospect, there seems no reason to doubt that the membership Association was formed to provide them channels for scholarly, nonpolitical activities that were not provided by the Institute, or for that matter by other organizations such as the American Oriental Society. It may be true that the majority of this group shared reasonably common political views about, for example, what American policy toward China ought to be. But the charge that the Association came into being for the purpose of serving as a convenient refuge for embattled Institute associates and that the Association as such promoted particular political views seems wholly unsupportable and unfair.

However harassed, the Institute of Pacific Relations was never indicted as a subversive organization; and the Association never suffered any direct organizational consequences of the Congressional hearings concerning the Institute. But the fact that many individual members of the Association were involved in the hearings had effects that never entirely disappeared. Most members simply did not want to become involved, personally or organizationally, in any kind of political entanglements of this sort, on either side. The determined nonpolitical posture of the Association was reinforced with the inclusion of South Asian specialists in 1955-56; they particularly wanted no part, however indirect, in any political controversies about revolutionary developments in China.

Extreme sensitivities about these matters were evident within the Association from its earliest years, and a series of awkward incidents resulted. The first of these was prompted by a letter of January 7, 1950, addressed to members of the Foreign Relations Committee of the Senate and the Foreign Affairs Committee of the House of Representatives by Charles S. Gardner, then President of the Association. As Gardner later explained the situation:

Having no present university connection, and desiring to convey quickly to busy men that I have some specialized knowledge of the Far East, I employed the Association letterhead. The first paragraph closed as follows. "The Far Eastern Association, of which I am at the moment head, is a strictly non-political national society of scholarship. Its members reflect all shades of opinion. As an individual citizen, however, I feel it my duty to present to you points of view which I find are largely shared by those colleagues whose knowledge and judgment I most highly respect."

Gardner's own summary of the "thesis" of his letter is as follows:

That the Kuomintang is hopelessly discredited; that the Chinese communists must compromise with their conservative countrymen, and convince them that they are free from foreign dictation; that Mao has no reason to love the Russians but, like Tito, will need strength to oppose them; and that we can better promote our national interests in China by making ourselves valuable to reconstruction there than by permitting Chiang to continue economic strangulation and bombardment of Chinese cities with American ships, planes and bombs.

When Gardner's letter became public knowledge, Director John A. Pope of the Freer Gallery initiated a proposal that the Association

immediately disavow it and request Gardner's resignation because his use of the Association's
letterhead for political activity disqualified
him both for office and for membership. Other
members of the leadership expressed concern "that
unless the Association writes a letter clarifying
the situation, we may be open to criticism on the
grounds that we have gone beyond the terms of our
constitution and may get in trouble with the
Internal Revenue Bureau in reference to our tax
exemption status which would be embarrassing to
all concerned." On March 6 Gardner wrote to the
Secretary reviewing and explaining what he had
done, concluding:

> If I have betrayed the confidence re-
> posed in me by my fellow members, I owe
> them apology and convey it now through
> you. In any event I recognize that use
> of the Association letterhead, even for
> a personal letter, on a political issue
> was a questionable procedure, and a doubt-
> ful precedent. I am herewith placing in
> your hands my resignation both as Presi-
> dent and as Member of the Association.
> Let me hasten to assure you, however,
> that acceptance of it will not in the
> slightest degree diminish my interest in
> the Association nor my continued desire
> to serve it in all ways which may lie
> within my power.

After voluminous correspondence passed among the
officers and Directors in a very short time,
Gardner's resignation was not accepted and the
controversy was terminated by Gardner's writing
a letter on March 31 to members of both Congressional committees, as follows:

> Gentlemen:
> On January 7 last I addressed to you a

letter presenting views on the subject
of American foreign policy in the Far
East, especially in China.

Although I stated in my first paragraph that I was writing as a private
citizen, my use of the letterhead of
this Association when writing on a political subject was improper. In point of
fact, no other member of the Association
collaborated with me in it, or was even
aware that I was writing it. Far less
does it represent in any manner an
"official" expression of the views of
the Association. This last would be
impossible because, in politics, it has
none. No political action of any kind
is contemplated in its Constitution.
On the contrary the latter states ex-
plicitly that:

"The objectives of the Association
shall be: (a) to form a scholarly,
non-political, and non-profit professional association of all persons
interested in the study of the Far
East; . . ."

I am now authorized and directed by
the officers and directors of the Far
Eastern Association officially to inform
you that (a) the Association disavows
and disassociates itself from any and
all opinions expressed in my letter, (b)
that the Association's policy is wholly
to abstain from political activity, and
(c) that it is taking action to prevent
its officers, directors, or other members from using its name, its letterhead,
or their connection with the Association
to support their personal political
views.

At its regular annual meeting that promptly

followed, the Board of Directors considered this matter closed. But minutes of the meeting add:

> In discussing the degree of discretion
> which the officers and directors have in
> the use of the Association's name and
> letterhead, it was agreed that a few
> words of caution by the Secretary at ap-
> propriate times would probably suffice
> to solve this problem. It was further
> agreed that members under various sorts
> of attack should be supported by other
> members on an individual basis, and that
> no action need be taken by the Associa-
> tion as an association, unless a member
> is attacked because of his affiliation
> with it.

The policy enunciated in Gardner's letter of March 31, 1950, governed the thinking of the leadership of the Association thereafter: "that the Association's policy is wholly to abstain from political activity."

Sensitivities about political matters caused an embarrassing controversy in planning the 1951 program, just when the troubles experienced by the Institute of Pacific Relations were reaching their greatest intensity. The Board of Direc-tors, at its 1950 meeting, had judged the 1951 meeting to be an appropriate time for discussion of the varied theories about the nature of Oriental societies that were then prominent in the thinking of the profession. Apparently without being aware of this, the Program Commit-tee for 1951, under the chairmanship of Hyman Kublin of Brooklyn, undertook independently to organize a session devoted to the subject. Kublin, working with a subcommittee on China comprising C. Martin Wilbur of Columbia and Marion Levy of Princeton, finally concluded that such a session could not be organized "properly"

70

and in early January, 1951, dropped it out of
the planned program. What had been planned was
a session involving Wittfogel, Lattimore, and
Wolfram Eberhard of Berkeley; but subsequently
Wittfogel's testimony before the Senate committee
hearing on the Institute of Pacific Relations
seems to have blocked the Program Committee's efforts to induce Lattimore and Eberhard to participate. When Wittfogel learned that the session
was not after all to be included in the program,
a University of Washington group protested that
personal and political considerations should not
influence the activities of the Association and
argued that the session should be scheduled even
if Wittfogel were the only formal speaker. The
Executive Committee supported the decision of
the Program Committee and insisted that no
political factors or implications were involved
in the decision. Suspicions and antagonisms
were exacerbated when Franz Michael of
Washington, scheduled to take part in a session
on reform and rebellion in modern China, submitted a title that the Program Committee judged
inappropriate. After voluminous exchanges of
correspondence between Seattle and various
officers of the Association and members of the
Program Committee, some members of the University
of Washington faculty withdrew from participation
in the 1951 meeting.

The Association's policy of abstaining from
political action did not deter the Board of
Directors and the business meetings from passing
resolutions in 1951 and in 1952 upholding
traditional principles of academic freedom
against real or threatened anti-intellectual re-
pression. In 1951 the Association officially
"deplored" action by the Regents of the University of California suspending or dismissing
faculty members considered Communist or pro-
Communist. In 1952, in the midst of the public
controversy about the Institute of Pacific

71

Relations, the Association went on record as follows:

Resolved that, whereas objective Far Eastern research and analysis are being endangered because of partisan attacks and the fear of later reprisals, the Far Eastern Association, as a non-political professional organization devoted to the scholarly study of the Far East:

1. *Affirms* its conviction that full freedom of expression for Far Eastern scholars as for others is an essential condition of effective professional work. Today the Far East is an area of immediate and critical national concern. Therefore we believe that in Far Eastern affairs there is a grave need for the reaffirmation and unimpaired maintenance of the free market place of ideas which is so vital a part of the American heritage of freedom and so important in the struggle against totalitarianism.

2. *Deplores* all activities of groups and individuals which work to enforce conformity and orthodoxy of opinion upon Far Eastern specialists. In particular we point to: a. attacks upon the motives and character of specialists simply because they hold or are alleged to have held views which are no longer popular or are not favored by the attackers; b. attempts to discredit individuals and research organizations without a properly substantiated basis of evidence or a full and balanced review of

the pertinent facts; c. attacks
upon Far Eastern specialists on
the basis of their association with
persons of widely varying political
views, when in fact such contacts
are essential to the professional
work of scholars, journalists, and
government workers; and d. arbi-
trary limitations upon the travel
of Far Eastern specialists.

The Secretary was instructed to communicate this
resolution to the presidents and trustees of all
American universities and colleges offering work
on the Far East, and he did so in a form letter
dated May 26, 1952.

In general, however, the Board of Directors
consistently avoided activities that might have
political complications. In 1953 *The Nation*
magazine obtained a membership list of the Association from the Secretariat for the purpose of
conducting a mail opinion poll of the membership
on American policies toward the Far East, assur-
ing "anonymity, etc." Members began protesting
as soon as the questionnaires were distributed,
and further inquiries revealed that *The Nation*
intended to assure the anonymity of individual
respondents but to identify them collectively as
members of the Association. The Association
then urged *The Nation* to stop this undertaking.
It did so, and results of the poll were not published.

In 1959 outgoing President Fairbank offered
a resolution to the business meeting to the
following effect:

The members present at the annual meeting of the Association for Asian Studies,
a non-political, professional academic organization devoted to scholarly study of
Asia, affirm the following propositions:

1. Scholarly study and understanding of all parts of Asia, including Communist areas, are a vital national need of the American people today, a necessary basis for the foreign relations of a democracy.
2. Scholarly study and understanding require maximum contact in all feasible forms. These forms include the flow of printed publications, travel for purposes of study including some exchange of persons, and above all a copious flow of information through news channels *not* limited to those of foreign countries.
3. In general, we affirm that scholarship demands unrestricted access to the widest possible flow of knowledge from all parts of Asia.

The Secretary is hereby requested to give this statement appropriate publicity.

Members present at the business meeting approved this resolution overwhelmingly, but the political ramifications of the action bothered some who had not been present when it was taken. Uneasiness about the matter led the Board in 1960 to establish a new policy concerning the submission of resolutions to the business meeting, to the effect that "any resolutions to be offered by officers should be cleared by the Executive Committee in advance. Anyone (members) wishing to offer a resolution should file it with the Secretary 24 hours ahead of the annual business meeting. . . ." Thus the Board tried to prevent the unanticipated submission of resolutions to the business meeting that might not receive the careful consideration they should get, in reference to the Association's policy about political involvements. In 1961 the Board tried to reinforce this policy when Theodore Herman of Colgate, complying with the new procedural rules, submitted to it, for later consideration at the business meeting, the following motion:

> I move that the Secretary send to President John F. Kennedy a letter expressing the approval of this Association, on grounds of principle as well as of national interest, for his efforts to remove from the government the power to delay or withhold the delivery of foreign printed matter to any person living within the United States, whether that person be a scholar or not.
> Also, that the Secretary be directed to give appropriate publicity to this letter of commendation as soon as possible.

The consensus of the Board, in discussing this motion, was that as an organization the Association should not take such action; but in the business meeting the motion was overwhelmingly adopted.

The Board was much more disturbed when the New York *Times* on March 21, 1966--just prior to the Association's annual meeting in New York City--published the full text of a controversial statement advocating open, free reconsideration of the American government's attitude toward and relations with the Chinese Communist government, which had been prepared by a private group and signed by 198 persons whom the *Times* in a front-page article about the statement identified as members of the Association. The Association's leadership reacted indignantly and quickly; a letter to the *Times* dated March 25 from Secretary L. A. P. Gosling insisted that the Association "was not involved in any way in the preparation, circulation or support of this statement" and added:

As a learned organization involving all
scholars specializing on Asia, of a great
range of political persuasion, the Association does not support any given policy
position. The meetings of the Association provide one of the few opportunities
for open discussion on all aspects of
Asia from all points of view, and as an
organization we are careful not to be
associated with any given policy position
so as to maintain this freedom and objec-
tivity.

Meantime, in other news stories and letters,
the Association's name had already been used in
reference to the China policy statement in ways
that many members considered most unfortunate;
and on March 23 the *Times* had worsened the situation by stating in an editorial that "The Statement on China by 198 Asian scholars—opposed by
only 19 other members of the Association for
Asian Studies—shows where the weight of informed
American opinion lies." At its meeting on April
3 the Board devoted much time to discussion of
this matter, and at the subsequent business meeting President Knight Biggerstaff read a detailed
explanation of the sequence of events leading up
to the unauthorized use of the membership list
by the China policy statement drafters and the
various mistaken statements about it that had
been appearing in the press. The business meeting endorsed the following reiteration of the
Association's policy in such matters: "Since the
Association for Asian Studies is a non-political
organization which is concerned only with the
scholarly study of Asia, the officers and directors deplore any use made of the Association's
name, intentionally or inadvertently, for any
other purpose."
During the middle 1960s, as America became
steadily more involved in war in Vietnam and as

relations between Communist China and the Soviet
Union deteriorated, American public opinion about
Asia altered, and repercussions were being increasingly felt by the Association in the late
1960s. A spreading commitment to "activism,"
especially among students, challenged the Association's traditional unaggressive posture regarding promotion of Asian Studies and particularly
raised new questions about the Association's
traditional dissociation from direct political
action. The Association for Asian Studies was
by no means alone in being affected by the new
activism. All learned societies were vulnerable
to challenges from their younger members. However, because so much of youthful activism was
related closely to the Vietnam war, the Association for Asian Studies was perhaps specially
vulnerable. The basic question was: Can a professional group in good conscience refuse to
take a stand on political questions of major
moral concern to society?

This challenge to the Association's tradition
first took significant shape in 1968 when a
group of its members organized a special meeting
to discuss America's involvement in Vietnam, in
conjunction with the annual meeting of the Association in Philadelphia. The Association's
leadership, anticipating that some sort of political activism would ensue, insisted that the
Vietnam meeting could not be conducted under
Association auspices or with any use of the
Association's name. Under instructions from the
Board, incoming President John W. Hall of Yale
read the following special statement at the
business meeting and issued it to the press:

> The Board of Directors of the Associ-
> ation for Asian Studies has repeatedly
> emphasized, and has asked me to emphasize
> publicly again, that this Association is
> a non-political organization whose

function is to promote the scholarly
study of Asia. This means that the Association for Asian Studies cannot endorse
any position regarding specific foreign
policy issues. It recognizes that its
members may wish to express their opinions on such issues. They do so, however, as private individuals and not in
the name of, or as spokesmen for, the
Association.

Although the "activists'" meeting was held during the course of the Association's annual meeting, it was held in separate facilities made
available by the University of Pennsylvania and
had no nominal relationship to the Association.
The participants were, however, overwhelmingly
Association members. They had a rather incon-
clusive meeting. But out of it grew a loose but
continuing organization calling itself the Committee of Concerned Asian Scholars (CCAS), dedicated to promoting political causes espoused by
its members, especially relating to the Vietnam
war. The organization exists as autonomous
chapters on various university campuses, commun-
icating with one another through two publications,
the *Bulletin of Concerned Asian Scholars* and the
CCAS Newsletter. By the beginning of 1970 CCAS
claimed thirteen chapters and a total active membership of approximately one thousand. It had
its first national conference in Boston in 1969
simultaneously with the annual meeting of the
Association for Asian Studies, some of whose
members found the CCAS program more interesting
than the Association's.

Gradually the commitment of CCAS clarified as
being a dedication "to fundamental changes in
the concept and purposes of current American
scholarship on Asia." The CCAS membership reportedly believes "that it is essential to com-
bine professional knowledge with moral and

political concerns." Thus CCAS comes into direct conflict with the traditional nonpolitical posture of the Association. During 1969 the Association's leadership watched with interest and concern as CCAS chapters debated possible future relationships with or roles within the Association. The Stanford CCAS chapter raised a crucial issue in asking, "Are the two organizations rivals?" Its own answer to the question was:

In the opinion of the Stanford chapter, these two organizations are indeed rivals and this relationship of rivalry, intellectual and political, is likely to continue over the next few years if not longer. We view the CCAS as differing from the AAS in its orientation toward political activism and moral scholarship as well as in its desire to bring professional responsibilities into harmony with our human responsibilities and in its democratic organization and practices. Furthermore, we believe that those members of the profession who oppose American cold war ideology and militaristic interventionism in Asia and elsewhere should give their primary loyalty, talents, and efforts to the CCAS rather than to the other organization, while those who can best be termed 'apolitical' or 'Cold warrior' scholars can hardly be expected to do so. In recognizing the past and continuing failures of our profession and the other professional organization, the AAS, to muster whatever expertise and political power Asian specialists in this country might have in opposition to the inhumane and barbaric attacks of the United States on Asian countries and cultures such as

those against the people of Viet-Nam, we
oppose attempts at reintegration with
the AAS until and unless CCAS members
and allies can take sufficient power to
insure the humanization and politiciza-
tion of the AAS to such degree as would
transform it into a democratic and anti-
imperialist organization similar to the
CCAS.

Although other CCAS chapters did not wholly support the Stanford chapter's position, it was
clear by early 1970 that CCAS posed more than a
trifling challenge to the Association for Asian
Studies and that the Association might be under
great pressure in the 1970s to transform itself
into a more aggressive organization, particularly
in political activity. The February, 1970,
issue of the *Newsletter* carried an appeal from
the Board of Directors with what "Cold Warriors"
in the membership would inevitably consider a
conciliatory tone:

The Board of Directors of the Association for Asian Studies deems it desirable
to record its views on the relationship
between the AAS and the Committee of Concerned Asian Scholars. The Committee
grew out of a meeting in Philadelphia
called by a number of scholars at the
time of the Association's annual meeting
in 1968. The Board of the AAS was
pleased with the arrangements at the
annual meeting in Boston in 1969 where
CCAS was provided with a table in the AAS
registration area. The holding of the
CCAS meeting in a near-by hotel enabled
members of both AAS and CCAS to participate in both meetings. The Board plans
to make similar arrangements at the
forthcoming annual AAS meeting in San

Francisco.

The Directors of the Association hope
that CCAS members will take an active
part in the AAS program at San Francisco.
For their part they see no incompatibil-
ity in scholars belonging to and being
active in both organizations. The Board
trusts that members of all persuasions
will feel that they can participate in
AAS activities without danger of compro-
mising their personal convictions or
political views. Thus, the Board hopes
that CCAS members, among others--identi-
fied as such if they wish--will take
part in our annual meetings. All
scholars concerned with Asian studies,
whatever their affiliation, must wrestle
with the problems of today. The Board
expects that these fundamental questions
can and will be discussed with candor
and mutual respect in San Francisco.

ORGANIZING FOR THE FUTURE

Reconsideration of all these varied aspects of
the Association's organization, functions, and
services was prompted by the great growth and expansion of the Association--and of the whole
Asian Studies profession--during the decade from
1958 to 1968. The remarkable extent of the Association's growth is suggested by an increase in
membership from 1,022 in 1958 to 3,752 in 1968;
an increase in circulation of the *Journal of
Asian Studies* from 1,954 to 6,002; an increase
in general-fund disbursements from $28,000 to
$128,000; and an increase in special-fund dis-
bursements from $65,000 to $160,000. Activity
within the profession at large was multiplying
during these years, in large part because of
special funding from the U.S. Office of Education, under terms of the National Defense Education Act of 1958, and from the Ford Foundation.
But growth of the Association probably exceeded
that of the profession at large. There was consequently no evidence that the Association was
threatened by failure or decline. There were,
however, widespread feelings that the Association was not organized effectively to cope with
the challenges and to seize the opportunities
that awaited it.
Such feelings were strongly expressed in the

annual report of Secretary Charles O. Hucker in the spring of 1967. In response to his urgings, the Board instructed incoming President Hall to appoint an ad hoc committee to study long-run organizational and procedural matters and report back to the Board in 1968. Such a committee, consisting of W. Theodore de Bary of Columbia, Richard Lambert of Pennsylvania, G. William Skinner of Stanford, Myron Weiner of the Massachusetts Institute of Technology, Hyman Kublin of Brooklyn, and Treasurer Hugh Patrick of Yale as well as Secretary Hucker and President Hall, met on March 8 and 9, 1968, in New York City. Its recommendations were submitted to the Board later that month at its regular meeting. The Board approved them in principle and appointed a small committee to study them carefully and transform them into a new Constitution and By-laws that could be distributed for vote of the membership. This ad hoc Committee on Organization and Functions comprised Hall, incoming President Holden Furber, Harry Benda of Yale, Rhoads Murphey of Michigan, de Bary, Weiner, and new Secretary David J. Steinberg. Its formal reorganizational proposals were submitted to the Board at its 1969 meeting, and the new Constitution and By-laws that it drafted were unanimously approved. In the autumn of 1969 the new Constitution and By-laws were approved overwhelmingly by the membership in a mail ballot, to become effective in 1970.

Reorganizing for the future thus became the principal preoccupation of Presidents Furber and de Bary and Secretary Steinberg during 1968 and 1969. Meanwhile, the Association's growth continued and accelerated. Between 1968 and 1970 membership increased further from 3,752 to 4,708; *Journal* circulation increased from 6,002 to 7,157; and from calendar years 1968 to 1969 general-fund revenues jumped from $129,000 to $153,000 and general-fund disbursements jumped from $128,000 to $145,000.

Reorganization took three principal paths: (1) strengthening the Secretariat to improve administration of the Association's affairs and to expand services, (2) restructuring governance of the Association to broaden membership participation in the leadership, and (3) a new activism on the part of the Association in promoting the Asian Studies profession and in serving the interests of its members.

The Association's Secretariat had long existed in cramped quarters at The University of Michigan with only two full-time employees, Mrs. Victoria Spang, as Manager, and a clerical assistant. The Secretary of the Association was drawn from the regular faculty of The University of Michigan and served the Association without compensation and without being released from any of his normal university duties. A second full-time clerical assistant to the Manager was added to help with the administrative burdens of 1966 and 1967, when the Secretariat served as the administrative agent of the 27th International Congress of Orientalists. She was retained thereafter in regular Association service; but at the same time, for personal reasons, Mrs. Spang had to reduce her accustomed full-time service and became part-time Manager. Secretary Hucker argued that the Secretariat's staffing situation was inadequate for maintaining the Association's basic daily-business routine and could not possibly undertake desirable new activities. Changes were authorized, and by 1970 the Secretariat enjoyed greatly expanded quarters provided by The University of Michigan. The staff of professional employees included Henry Richmond as Administrative Secretary and William Green as Manager, with Mrs. Spang continuing on part-time duty with the new title of Comptroller. The Secretary of the Association, who had overall responsibility for the functioning of the

Secretariat, while not released from any of his university duties, was receiving an annual stipend of $1,500 from the Association. Active discussion had even developed about transforming the Secretaryship into a full-time professional Executive Secretaryship. Also, a grant from the McGregor Fund of Detroit had made it possible to plan automation of the Secretariat's record-keeping procedures and to publish an automated directory of the membership, possibly in 1971.

The Constitution and By-laws that became effective in 1970 alter the Association's structure of governance more substantially than any other change since its beginning. Minor changes include abolition of the former Second Vice Presidency and consolidation of the former office of Treasurer with that of the Secretary, into a new office of Secretary-Treasurer. The Finance Committee, Publications Committee, and Advisory Council on Research and Development remain essentially as before, as do the Association's various publications. But the Board of Directors has been transformed into an umbrella-like governing superstructure supervising (and with its own membership constituted mostly out of) four new elected area councils: a Council on South Asia, a Council on Southeast Asia, a Council on China and Inner Asia, and a Council on Northeast Asia. The new area councils become the principal liaison agencies between the Association and the membership, and it is prescribed that each council (and, through the councils, the Board itself) shall have roughly equal representation of historians, social scientists, and humanists. Each council, directly elected by its own "area clientele" and with a balanced representation among disciplinary interests, is now charged with principal responsibility for reviewing, promoting, and developing the Association's and the profession's activities and interests affecting its geographic area. It is anticipated that this new structure, though somewhat more elaborate than its forerunner and involving more complicated electoral procedures, will make it easier for the individual member to find a focal point for his interests (the area council), will make obsolete some of the former special-interest and developmental committees of the Association, and will provide for more vigorous developmental initiatives in closer touch with the problems and interests of the members. It is also anticipated that the new structure will make it possible for the Association, through the area councils, to represent the profession authoritatively before the academic world generally, foundations and government agencies, and perhaps even the general public. Whether or not the new structure will fulfill all these expectations will depend on the quality and effort of the persons nominated for and elected to the area councils, acceptance of the area councils' leadership roles both within and outside the Association, and supporting services made available to the Board and the area councils by the expanded Secretariat.

The strengthening of the Secretariat staff and a more activist outlook among the leaders of the Association combined to involve the Association in a number of new promotional and developmental activities and services by 1970. The Association had begun offering its members highly successful summer round-trip flights to Japan, cooperating with the United States Employment Service (after a lapse of more than a decade) to provide job-placement services at its annual meetings, taking on legal sponsorship of educational tours for Americans in Asia and for Asians in America, and, in its *Newsletter*, providing Professional Personnel Registry services and regular lists of dissertations recently completed or in progress. Moreover, the

Association had reversed its traditional policy,
reiterated as late as 1967, "that projects using
government funds must be administered by an
institution other than this Association." In
1968, when the Committee on Southeast Asia reported on its progress in setting up an inter-
university committee to seek substantial
government funding for a variety of projects,
the Board urged the Committee "to come to AAS as
a fund-administering and project-encouraging
organization rather than a university or other
non-profit organization." And in 1969 the
Association sought and obtained, or otherwise
accepted, a three-year grant from the National
Science Foundation to support automation of the
annual *Bibliography of Asian Studies*, a U.S.
Office of Education grant to support a Language
and Area Studies Review being conducted principally by Richard Lambert of Pennsylvania,
and a U.S. Office of Education grant to support
two conferences on Asian Studies in American
Secondary Education--in the latter case reviv-
ing a long-dormant interest of the Association.

Thus with a more flexible, representative,
and responsive leadership structure, with a
strengthened Secretariat, with a new commitment
to active promotion and development of the
Asian Studies profession, and with concerned
cordiality toward the advocates of "politici-
zation" within its membership, the Association
for Asian Studies begins the 1970s with both a
new look and a new outlook. That it has had a
successful existence to date is evidenced by
its continually growing membership and its continually expanding services and activities.
Its prospects for the future would seem to depend in considerable part on how successfully
its new structure and attitudes can accommodate
and vitalize the interests of the older generation of scholars who have guided Asian Studies
to this point and the younger generation into
whose hands the profession is passing.

APPENDICES

APPENDIX 1

DATA ON CONSTITUTION AND BY-LAWS
OF THE AAS

Successive versions of the Association's Constitution and By-laws can be found as follows:

1. The original version was published in *The Far Eastern Quarterly*, VII (August, 1948), 410-418.

2. The revision of 1956 was published in *The Journal of Asian Studies*, XVI (August, 1957), 679-688, together with a brief history of the Association.

3. The 1962 version was published in *The Journal of Asian Studies*, XXII (May, 1963), 366-372; and was reprinted together with a brief twenty-year history of the Association in volume XXVIII (November, 1968), 201-241.

4. The version becoming effective in 1970 was published as a November, 1969, supplementary issue of the Association's *Newsletter*.

Annual reports of the Association were normally published in the August issues of the *Journal* until 1969, when they began being published in October issues of the *Newsletter*.

91

APPENDIX 2

MEMBERSHIP MEETINGS OF THE AAS, 1948-1970

Year	Site	Special Circumstances
1948	New York: Columbia University	Organizational meeting
1949	New Haven: Yale University	With American Oriental Society
1950	Ann Arbor: University of Michigan	
1951	Philadelphia	With American Oriental Society
1952	Cambridge: Harvard University	With American Oriental Society
1953	Cleveland	With Association of American Geographers
1954	New York	With American Oriental Society
1955	Washington	
1956	Philadelphia	
1957	Boston	
1958	New York	With American Oriental Society

Year	Site	Special Circumstances
1959	Washington	
1960	New York	With American Oriental Society
1961	Chicago	
1962	Boston	Concurrently, but not jointly, with American Oriental Society
1963	Philadelphia	
1964	Washington	
1965	San Francisco	
1966	New York	
1967	Chicago	
1968	Philadelphia	
1969	Boston	
1970	San Francisco	

93

APPENDIX 3

LEADERSHIP OF THE AAS, 1948-1970

AAS Presidents

1948-49
  Arthur W. Hummel
1949-50
  Charles S. Gardner
1950-51
  Harold S. Quigley
1951-52
  Robert B. Hall
1952-53
  Rupert Emerson
1953-54
  Felix M. Keesing
1954-55
  Kenneth S. Latourette
1955-56
  Edwin O. Reischauer
1956-57
  L. Carrington Goodrich
1957-58
  Hugh Borton
1958-59
  John K. Fairbank
1959-60
  George B. Cressey
1960-61
  W. Norman Brown
1961-62
  Lauriston Sharp
1962-63
  Earl H. Pritchard
1963-64
  William W. Lockwood
1964-65
  Arthur F. Wright
1965-66
  Knight Biggerstaff

1966-67
  Karl J. Pelzer
1967-68
  John W. Hall
1968-69
  Holden Furber
1969-70
  W. Theodore de Bary

AAS Secretaries

1948-49
  Wilma Fairbank
1949-50
  Joseph Yamagiwa
1950-52
  Knight Biggerstaff
1952-53
  Robert E. Ward
1953-59
  Ronald Anderson
1959-61
  Robert I. Crane
1961-63
  Russell H. Fifield
1963-66
  L. A. Peter Gosling
1966-68
  Charles O. Hucker
1968-70
  David J. Steinberg

AAS Treasurers

1948-51
  Hugh Borton
1951-54
  C. Martin Wilbur

1954-61
  Hyman Kublin
1961-64
  Eugene Langston
1964-70
  Hugh T. Patrick

AAS Journal Editors

1948-51
  Earl H. Pritchard

1951-55
  Arthur F. Wright
1955-59
  Donald Shively
1959-62
  Roger F. Hackett
1962-65
  Rhoads Murphey
1965-70
  Robert I. Crane

AAS Board of Directors

Except for inaugural year of the Association, Board members serve for three consecutive years. Date indicated is year of election.

1948-Raymond Kennedy
      Virginia Thompson
      Ssu-Yü Teng
      Woodbridge Bingham
      John A. Pope
      C. Martin Wilbur
      William W. Lockwood
      James M. Menzies
      George E. Taylor

1949-George B. Cressey
      William L. Holland
      Owen Lattimore

1950-George E. Taylor
      Edwin O. Reischauer
      Robert Hall
      John F. Embree

1951-Woodbridge Bingham
      Clarence Hamilton
      John E. Orchard
      Lauriston Sharp
      Laurence Sickman

1952-Shannon McCune
      Karl J. Pelzer
      Donald Shively
      Joseph Yamagiwa

1953-Edwin G. Beal
      Schuyler Van Cammann
      Earl H. Pritchard

1954-Marius B. Jansen
      Cora duBois
      E. A. Kracke

1955-Robert E. Ward
      Arthur F. Wright
      Lien-sheng Yang

1956-W. Norman Brown
      William W. Lockwood
      H. Arthur Steiner

1957-Y. R. Chao
      Richard L. Park
      Alexander C. Soper
      Frank N. Trager

1958-Norton S. Ginsburg
      Virginia Thompson
      C. Martin Wilbur
      Robert Hall

1959-John F. Cady
      Douglas G. Haring
      Daniel H. H. Ingalls
      Chitoshi Yanaga

1960—James R. Hightower
    Charles O. Hucker
    Robert A. Scalapino
    Milton B. Singer

1961—William Theodore de Bary
    Alexander Eckstein
    John A. Harrison
    Lucian Pye

1962—A. Doak Barnett
    Richard K. Beardsley
    Robert I. Crane
    G. William Skinner

1963—Robert Blum
    James T. C. Liu
    James W. Morley
    Henry Rosovsky

1964—Wing-tsit Chan
    George M. Kahin
    Richard D. Lambert
    Shunzo Sakamaki

1965—Fred Eggan
    Joseph R. Levenson
    Herbert Passin
    Benjamin Schwartz

1966—Roger F. Hackett
    Richard H. Robinson
    Myron Weiner
    Lien-sheng Yang

1967—Harry J. Benda
    Morris D. Morris
    Rhoads Murphey
    Glenn P. Paige

1968—Derk Bodde
    Clifford Geertz
    Ping-ti Ho
    Thomas C. Smith

1969—Robert Bellah
    Jerome A. Cohen
    Ainslie Embree
    Edwin G. Pulleyblank

APPENDIX 4

PUBLICATIONS

Publications of the AAS

The Journal of Asian Studies, 1941–
Published quarterly in November, February, May,
and August. Until 1956 known as *The Far
Eastern Quarterly*.
Special issue:
June, 1964 (volume XXIII): *Aspects of Religion
in South Asia*, edited by E. B. Harper.
Papers delivered at a 1961 research conference sponsored by the Association's Committee
on South Asia. Also published separately as
a book by the University of Washington Press,
1965.
Bibliography of Asian Studies, 1956–
Published annually in September as a fifth issue
of *The Journal of Asian Studies*. Originated
as a separate publication, *Bulletin of Far
Eastern Bibliography* under the editorship of
Earl H. Pritchard (volumes 1-5, 1936-40),
then incorporated into *The Far Eastern
Quarterly* from 1941 through 1955, as an
annual compilation beginning in 1949.
Newsletter of the Association for Asian Studies,
1955–
Published quarterly.
Special issues:
December, 1963 (volume IX): *Paperbound Books on
Asia*.
September, 1964 (volume X): *Guide to Asian
Studies in Undergraduate Education*.
September, 1966 (volume XI): *Paperbound Books on*

Asia.

April, 1967 (volume XII): *Asian Studies under the National Defense Education Act.*

September, 1968 (volume XIII): *Reprints and Microform Materials in Asian Studies.*

November, 1969 (volume XV): *Proposed Constitution of the Association for Asian Studies, Inc.*

Monographs and Papers

Published by J. J. Augustin Publisher, Locust Valley, New York, until 1963 and thereafter by the University of Arizona Press, Tucson, except as otherwise indicated.

I. *Money Economy in Medieval Japan* by Delmer M. Brown (1951).

II. *China's Management of the American Barbarians* by Earl Swisher (1951).

III. *Leadership and Power in the Chinese Community of Thailand* by G. William Skinner (1958). Cornell University Press.

IV. *Siam Under Rama III, 1824-1851* by Walter F. Vella (1957).

V. *The Rise of the Merchant Class in Tokugawa Japan, 1600-1868* by Charles David Sheldon (1958).

VI. *Chinese Secret Societies in Malaya* by L. F. Comber (1959).

VII. *The Traditional Chinese Clan Rules* by Hui-chen Wang Liu (1959).

VIII. *A Comparative Analysis of the Jajmani System* by Thomas O. Beidelman (1959).

IX. *Colonial Labor Policy and Administration* by J. Norman Parmer (1959).

X. *Bankghuad--A Community Study in Thailand* by Howard Keva Kaufman (1959).

XI. *Agricultural Involution, the Processes of Ecological Change in Indonesia* by Clifford Geertz (1963). University of California Press.

XII. *The Maharastha Purana* by Edward C. Dimock, Jr. and Pratul Chandra Gupta (1965). East-

West Center Press.

XIII. *Conciliation and Japanese Law: Tokugawa and Modern* by Dan Henderson (1965). University of Washington Press.

XIV. *The Malayan Tin Industry to 1914* by Wong Lin Ken (1965).

XV. *Reform, Rebellion, and the Heavenly Way* by Benjamin Weems (1965).

XVI. *Korean Literature: Topics and Themes* by Peter H. Lee (1965).

XVII. *Ch'oe Pu's Diary: A Record of Drifting Across the Sea* by John Meskill (1965).

XVIII. *The British in Malaya--The First Forty Years (1786-1826)* by K. G. Tregonning (1965).

XIX. *Chiaraijima Village: Land Tenure, Taxation & Local Trade* by William Chambliss (1965).

XX. *Shinran's Gospel of Pure Grace* by Alfred Bloom (1965).

XXI. *Before Aggression* by Ernst Presseisen (1965).

XXII. *A Documentary Chronicle of Sino-Western Relations 1644-1820* by Lo Shu Fu (1966).

XXIII. *K'ang Yu-wei: A Biography and a Symposium* by Jung-pang Lo (1967).

XXIV. *Restoration of Thailand Under Rama I, 1782-1809* by Klaus Wenk (1968).

XXV. *Political Centers and Cultural Regions in Early Bengal* by B. Morrison (1969).

XXVI. *The Peasant Rebellions of the Late Ming Dynasty* by James Bunyan Parsons (1968).

Publications Sponsored by AAS Committees

Committee on Chinese Thought (1951-1962)

Studies in Chinese Thought edited by Arthur F. Wright. University of Chicago Press, 1953. Paperbound edition, 1969.

Chinese Thought and Institutions edited by John K. Fairbank. University of Chicago Press, 1957. Paperbound edition, 1967.

Confucianism in Action edited by David S.

Nivison and Arthur F. Wright. Stanford
University Press, 1959. Paperbound edition, 1969.

The Confucian Persuasion edited by Arthur F.
Wright. Stanford University Press, 1960.
Paperbound edition, 1969.

Confucian Personalities edited by Arthur F.
Wright and Denis Twitchett. Stanford University Press, 1962. Paperbound edition,
1969.

Confucianism and Chinese Civilization edited
by Arthur F. Wright. Atheneum Press, 1964.
(A selection of articles from the five
aforementioned volumes.)

Conference on Modern Japan (1961-1968)

*Changing Japanese Attitudes Toward Moderniza-
tion* edited by Marius B. Jansen. Princeton
University Press, 1965.

The State and Economic Enterprise in Japan
edited by William W. Lockwood. Princeton
University Press, 1965.

Aspects of Political Change in Modern Japan
edited by Ronald P. Dore. Princeton University Press, 1967.

Political Development in Modern Japan edited
by Robert E. Ward. Princeton University
Press, 1968.

Committee on South Asia

*Resources for South Asian Language Studies in
the United States* by W. Norman Brown. University of Pennsylvania Press, 1961.

*Resources for South Asian Area Studies in the
United States* by Richard D. Lambert. University of Pennsylvania Press, 1962.

Tagore Memorial Lectureship Committee (1961-1968)

Sanskrit Poetics as a Study of Aesthetics by
S. K. De. University of California Press,
1963.

Social Change in Modern India by M. N.
Srinivas. University of California Press,
1966.

Man in the Universe: Some Cultural Continuities in India by W. Norman Brown. University of California Press, 1966.

Studies in Gupta Art by Moti Chandra. In press.

South Asia Microform Committee

South Asian Library and Research Notes, 1964–
Originally distributed as a committee newsletter; in 1967 altered to be issued separately and/or jointly with *The Quarterly Review of Historical Studies* (Calcutta).

Committee on State Politics in India

State Politics in India edited by Myron Weiner. Princeton University Press, 1967.

Committee on Southeast Asia

Southeast Asia: Problems of U.S. Policy edited by William Henderson. M.I.T. Press, 1963.

Inter–university Southeast Asia Committee

International Biographical Directory of Southeast Asia Specialists edited by Robert O. Tilman, 1969.

Committee on East Asian Libraries

Newsletter, 1963–
Published three or more times a year for selective distribution.

Ming Biographical History Project

Draft Ming Biographies, 1964–
Published irregularly for selective distribution.

Chinese Language Teachers Association

Journal of the Chinese Language Teachers Association, 1966–
Published three times a year in February, May, and November.

Association of Teachers of Japanese

Journal-Newsletter of the Association of Teachers of Japanese, 1963–
Published three times a year.

Other Publications

Ministers of Modernization: Elite Mobility in the Meiji Restoration edited by Bernard S. Silberman. University of Arizona Press, 1964. Papers from a 1963 research conference partly sponsored by the Association.

APPENDIX 5

GROWTH OF THE AAS MEMBERSHIP, 1949-1970

Year	Regular Members	Supporting Members	Honorary Members	Life Members	Student Members	Associate Members	Total
1949	563(?)	17	...	...	...	?	606
1950	?	?	?	?	?	?	689
1951	?	?	?	?	?	?	727
1952	682	25	...	1	...	...	747
1953	722	15	6	1	...	6	773
1954	681	22	7	1	...	7	734
1955	696	30	6	1	...	6	763
1956	837	36	6	2	...	6	903
1957	886	51	5	4	...	5	970
1958	938	45	5	4	...	5	1,022
1959	1,037	35	5	9	...	38	1,124
1960	1,061	57	5	11	364	34	1,532
1961	1,297	29	5	14	305	29	1,679
1962	1,470	35	6	16	454	29	2,010
1963	1,584	52	6	17	665	31	2,355
1964	1,772	40	5	19	762	29	2,637
1965	2,089	23	4	19	899	50	3,084
1966	2,241	31	5	23	993	48	3,341
1967	2,475	7	4	23	1,034	43	3,586
1968	2,550	6	4	24	1,138	30	3,752
1969	2,734	6	4	24	1,394	45	4,207
1970	3,258	6	4	24	1,332	84	4,708

Notes:
   Figures reflect membership data as of March in the years indicated.
   Norman Dwight Harris was considered a Patron member from 1949 through 1958.
   Special category for student memberships was not created until 1960.

APPENDIX 6

PROFESSIONAL FIELDS OF THE AAS MEMBERSHIP, 1953–1970
(all figures are percentages)

Year	Anthropology	Art	Economics	Far East	Geography	History	Journalism	Language & Literature	Law	Religion & Philosophy	Political Science	Sociology	Other & Unknown
1953	5.8	4.5	4.7	5.4	4.1	22.9	...	11.9	...	2.1	17.7	2.1	18.8
1954	5.7	4.3	3.5	3.2	3.6	24.2	...	10.5	...	3.6	20.0	2.7	18.7
1955	5.5	4.2	4.1	3.8	3.8	25.3	...	10.5	...	3.4	20.0	2.4	17.0
1956	7.4	3.8	5.4	3.2	3.7	23.0	...	9.5	...	3.1	20.5	3.7	16.7
1957	8.6	3.7	5.3	2.8	3.8	23.3	...	9.7	...	2.6	20.5	3.2	16.5
1958	8.3	3.8	5.4	1.9	4.0	24.6	...	8.2	.4	2.5	19.2	3.1	18.6
1959	8.0	2.8	4.6	1.9	3.2	24.1	.2	7.5	.6	2.9	17.2	2.8	21.0
1960	7.0	2.4	5.4	1.8	3.3	24.7	.2	7.0	.8	3.2	18.1	3.0	23.0
1961	6.7	3.1	5.5	3.3	3.7	24.0	.7	7.8	1.4	4.7	18.9	3.6	16.6
1962	6.7	2.8	5.3	3.0	3.4	23.6	.6	7.7	1.3	4.4	18.5	3.6	19.1
1963	7.0	2.6	5.5	2.8	3.1	25.0	.6	9.5	1.1	4.5	18.9	2.9	16.5
1964	7.3	2.5	5.6	2.8	3.0	25.0	.6	9.3	1.1	4.5	18.8	3.5	16.0
1965	7.4	2.3	4.7	2.9	3.2	26.5	.4	10.3	1.0	4.5	19.3	3.1	14.4
1966	7.2	2.3	4.7	2.8	3.3	27.2	.4	9.5	.9	4.6	19.3	3.3	14.5
1967	7.0	2.1	4.3	2.7	2.9	27.6	.6	9.0	.9	4.3	18.9	3.1	16.6
1968	6.8	1.9	4.6	3.0	3.0	28.9	.4	9.3	.8	4.2	19.6	3.2	14.3
1969	6.5	1.9	4.1	2.6	2.6	28.7	.4	9.0	.9	4.4	18.0	3.0	17.9
1970	5.9	1.9	4.3	2.6	2.5	25.7	.4	9.2	.4	4.5	17.5	3.0	20.8
Average	7.2	3.0	5.0	2.9	3.4	24.9	.4	8.9	.9	3.7	19.1	3.0	17.4

Note: Average based on twelve-year sample, 1956–1967, except Law (1958–1967).

APPENDIX 7

AREA INTERESTS OF THE AAS MEMBERSHIP, 1953–1970
(all figures are percentages)

Year[a]	General Far East	China	Japan	Southeast Asia	South Asia	Central Asia	Korea	East Asia	Unknown	Statistical Error + Other[b]
1953	29.5	26.6	16.2	14.7		1.1	.9	...	10.5	.5
1954	24.7	26.1	16.6	16.7		.4	2.2	...	10.5	2.4
1955	26.4	26.1	18.2	15.7		.8	1.6	...	8.6	1.1
1956	20.9	23.1	16.0	13.1	12.0	1.1	1.5	...	8.4	2.4
1957	21.0	21.6	15.3	14.2	12.5	1.9	1.4	...	9.2	1.7
1958	15.3	26.3	17.9	13.0	13.1	1.2	1.6	...	10.1	.1
1959	8.1	27.7	17.3	14.2	10.4	.9	1.4	2.1	15.4	.4
1960	8.2	25.1	15.6	13.2	13.8	.6	1.2	1.6	15.8	.9
1961	8.9	18.3	13.2	15.4	13.5	2.1	1.0	10.1	13.0	2.3
1962	8.7	17.8	13.3	15.2	13.7	1.7	.8	9.4	14.7	1.3
1963	[Unavailable]									
1964	8.3	20.1	12.8	14.4	14.9	1.3	.8	9.9	12.7	.8
1965	8.8	20.5	12.8	15.1	15.5	1.2	1.0	8.5	11.0	1.6
1966	8.5	22.1	12.6	14.8	15.6	1.1	1.1	8.5	10.9	.9
1967	8.6	22.9	12.1	14.1	15.2	.9	.8	8.5	12.1	1.0
1968	8.7	24.8	12.5	14.3	15.6	.7	.8	8.6	9.8	.7
1969	7.8	23.7	11.7	14.0	15.1	.8	.9	8.3	12.1	1.9
1970	9.4	21.9	12.0	13.4	13.9	.5	.9	7.8	15.2	5.0

[a]Year runs from April to March of the following year.

[b]"Other" includes such geographic regions as Russian Asia, Northeast Asia, Middle East, Mongolia, Muslim world.

APPENDIX 8

AAS MEMBERSHIP TRENDS BY U.S. REGIONS, 1953–1970
(all figures are percentages)[a]

Year[b]	New England[c]	Middle Atlantic	East North Central	East South Central	West South Central	West North Central	South Atlantic	Mountain	Pacific
1953	14.3	24.7	15.8	.6	1.3	3.9	17.8	1.2	18.8
1954	14.0	25.9	15.8	.9	1.0	3.1	15.5	1.7	21.0
1955	12.2	30.3	13.3	.5	1.0	3.7	14.2	1.6	21.8
1956	11.3	28.7	13.9	.6	.8	3.7	15.5	1.6	23.2
1957	12.6	27.5	14.1	.6	.8	3.6	14.1	1.6	23.9
1958	13.4	28.1	14.1	.4	1.3	4.1	14.1	1.4	23.0
1959	12.5	28.3	15.3	.7	.9	3.5	14.9	1.5	21.8
1960	12.1	26.5	14.9	.6	1.5	4.4	16.1	2.1	21.1
1961	12.9	26.1	16.1	.7	1.6	4.9	14.9	2.3	20.2
1962	13.0	25.6	18.4	.7	1.6	4.8	13.6	2.4	19.9
1963	15.5	25.6	16.3	.6	1.5	4.7	13.4	2.3	18.6
1964	12.2	27.0	16.4	.8	1.6	4.8	14.8	2.9	17.9
1965	11.3	24.0	16.0	.8	1.5	5.0	15.4	3.3	22.6
1966	10.6	22.5	16.8	1.0	1.4	5.3	14.4	3.1	24.6
1967	10.5	23.5	17.3	1.2	1.5	5.3	14.6	2.8	22.9
1968	10.3	23.9	18.1	1.2	1.8	5.8	12.8	2.9	23.1
1969	11.4	23.3	18.1	1.0	1.8	5.5	13.1	2.9	22.6
1970	11.1	23.0	18.8	1.2	1.8	5.7	12.8	3.2	22.1

[a]Accuracy is within 1.5% of 100.0%.

[b]Membership year runs from April to March of the following year.

[c]For explanation of areas see Appendix 13.

FOREIGN MEMBERS AND SUBSCRIBERS, 1953-1970

Non-member Subscriptions

Year	1953	1954	1955	1956	1957	1958	1959	1960	1961	1962	1963	1964	1965	1966	1967	1968	1969	1970
Africa	3	3	2	...	4	...	3	5	6	6	7	8	9	10	12	11	14	12
Asia	130	113	336	...	358	...	357	448	497	525	550	568	598	597	554	483	450	460
Canada	5	9	8	...	12	...	9	13	13	16	20	40	31	36	46	53	58	63
Europe	74	72	82	...	94	...	100	114	145	128	111	145	157	179	193	172	216	218
Latin Am.	...	...	...	...	...	...	...	2	1	5	4	4	5	3	5	7	6	6
ME/NE	...	1	3	...	5	...	3	4	5	5	7	8	10	8	11	10	11	14
Slavic	12	12	8	...	17	...	21	19	17	21	28	28	14	21	20	22	24	128

Membership

Year	1953	1954	1955	1956	1957	1958	1959	1960	1961	1962	1963	1964	1965	1966	1967	1968	1969	1970
Africa	...	...	...	...	...	1	1	1	2	2	2	1	2	2	5	6	3	4
Asia	44	45	49	61	69	76	73	97	105	119	138	169	198	197	200	211	218	243
Canada	11	7	6	8	9	12	16	17	23	28	30	36	49	67	80	96	118	149
Europe	21	20	21	16	15	13	22	34	36	41	47	72	63	76	80	85	87	77
Latin Am.	1	...	1	...	1	...	3	2	1	2	2	2	4	3	4	8	7	5
ME/NE	1	...	1	...	1	...	3	5	3	3	3	3	3	8	6	6	8	8
Slavic	...	...	...	...	...	...	...	...	...	...	...	...	...	...	...	...	...	...

APPENDIX 10

ANNUAL PERCENTAGE INCREASE OF SELECTED AREA INTERESTS OF AAS MEMBERS, 1959–1969

Year	1959	1960	1961	1962	1963	1964	1965	1966	1967	1968	1969	Average	Net
General Far East	base year	40.0	18.6	16.0	NA[a]	base year	23.8	5.5	8.3	8.1	1.0	15.0	274.0
China	"	24.7	-24.6	16.2	"	"	23.4	12.2	11.4	13.1	7.8	10.5	230.0
Japan	"	23.1	- 6.8	21.1	"	"	16.1	7.7	2.2	8.3	3.4	9.3	157.0
South East Asia	"	29.3	27.2	18.1	"	"	23.2	6.1	1.4	6.1	10.4	15.2	280.0
South Asia	"	80.0	8.1	21.1	"	"	21.2	9.3	5.2	7.1	8.5	11.5[b]	455.0

[a]NA = statistics not available.

[b]This average excludes the 80% increase of 1959–1960.

APPENDIX 11

AAS MEMBERSHIP COMPOSITE, 1953–1970
(all figures are percentages)

| | Membership | | Non-member Journal | | Membership Breakdown | | |
	Domestic	Foreign	Domestic	Foreign	Regular	Student[b]	Other
Year[a]							
1953	90.2	9.8	65.9	33.1			
1954	90.0	10.0	68.4	31.6			
1955	89.5	10.5	52.7	47.3			
1956	89.6	10.4	56.8	43.2			
1957	90.3	9.7	51.5	48.5			
1958	88.9	11.1	56.3	43.7			
1959	89.5	10.5	58.3	41.7			
1960	89.6	10.4	50.0	50.0	69.4	23.8	6.8
1961	89.9	10.1	53.4	46.6	77.4	18.3	4.3
1962	90.0	10.0	51.8	48.2	73.2	22.1	4.7
1963	90.5	9.5	51.7	48.3	67.6	28.5	3.9
1964	89.3	10.7	52.2	47.8	67.5	28.9	3.3
1965	89.6	10.4	54.3	45.7	67.2	29.4	3.3
1966	89.2	10.8	57.9	42.1	67.2	29.3	3.7
1967	89.5	10.5	61.4	38.6	69.6	28.3	2.5
1968	89.2	10.8	62.4	37.6	67.3	30.3	2.4
1969	88.3	11.7	65.4	34.6	64.4	33.6	1.9
1970	89.4	10.6	63.5	36.5	70.4	28.8	.7

[a]Membership year runs from April to March of the following year.

[b]Student membership did not begin until 1960; it includes retirees and people in military service.

APPENDIX 12

CIRCULATION OF THE FAR EASTERN QUARTERLY/JOURNAL OF ASIAN STUDIES, 1949–1970

Year	Total Circulation
1949	1,129
1950	1,238
1951	1,340
1952	1,387
1953	1,449
1954	1,423
1955	1,692
1956	1,774
1957	1,980
1958	1,954
1959	2,115
1960	2,801
1961	3,052
1962	3,480
1963	3,928
1964	4,312
1965	4,890
1966	5,366
1967	5,762
1968	6,002
1969	6,466
1970	7,157

Note: Figures given are approximate circulation figures for March of the year indicated.

APPENDIX 13

TRENDS IN NON-MEMBER CIRCULATION OF THE JOURNAL OF ASIAN STUDIES
BY U.S. REGIONS, 1953-1970 [a]
(all figures are percentages)

Year[b]	Northeast	Middle Atlantic	East North Central	East South Central	West South Central	West North Central	South Atlantic	Mountain	Pacific
1953	9.7	28.1	11.9	2.9	4.5	7.7	16.4	3.1	14.8
1954	9.6	25.8	12.3	2.7	5.0	9.8	15.1	2.9	17.6
1955	8.9	26.3	12.0	3.2	4.9	8.1	16.7	2.8	17.1
1956	[Unavailable]								
1957	8.4	29.0	12.5	2.7	5.2	7.5	14.7	2.8	16.5
1958	[Unavailable]								
1959	8.1	27.0	13.3	2.8	4.8	7.7	16.2	2.9	16.4
1960	8.7	25.5	13.5	2.6	4.6	7.2	16.5	3.1	17.5
1961	8.9	24.7	14.7	2.6	4.4	7.3	16.0	2.9	17.8
1962	8.5	24.2	14.8	2.3	4.3	7.5	16.2	3.0	18.0
1963	8.4	23.8	14.8	2.3	4.4	7.8	16.7	2.9	17.9
1964	8.0	23.2	14.3	2.8	4.1	7.9	16.7	2.9	19.0
1965	8.9	23.5	13.2	2.9	2.9	8.0	18.0	3.6	20.1
1966	8.5	24.4	15.6	3.3	4.6	7.8	15.6	3.5	16.6
1967	8.6	22.9	14.3	2.8	4.3	8.0	17.2	3.2	18.5
1968	8.6	22.7	14.6	2.9	4.8	8.1	17.0	3.2	17.7
1969	8.5	22.1	14.8	3.3	4.8	7.9	17.7	2.9	17.3
1970	7.2	22.5	14.1	3.6	4.3	8.0	18.1	3.1	17.1

[a]Accuracy is within 1.5% of 100.0%.

[b]Membership year runs from April to the following March.

Northeast	Middle Atlantic	West South Central	West North Central	East North Central
Connecticut	New Jersey	Arkansas	Iowa	Indiana
Maine	New York	Louisiana	Kansas	Illinois
Massachusetts	Pennsylvania	Oklahoma	Minnesota	Michigan
New Hampshire		Texas	Missouri	Ohio
Rhode Island			Nebraska	Wisconsin
Vermont			N. & S. Dakota	

East South Central	South Atlantic	Mountain	Pacific
Alabama	Delaware	Arizona	Alaska
Kentucky	District of Columbia	Colorado	California
Mississippi	Florida	Idaho	Hawaii
Tennessee	Georgia	Montana	Oregon
	Maryland	Nevada	Washington
	N. & S. Carolina	New Mexico	Canal Zone
	Virginia	Utah	Guam
	West Virginia	Wyoming	Puerto Rico
			Virgin Islands
			Wake

APPENDIX 14

DIVISION BY AREA OF ARTICLES PUBLISHED IN
THE JOURNAL OF ASIAN STUDIES
(all figures are percentages of N)

Volume	Asia (incl. Central)	South Asia	Southeast Asia	China	India	Japan & Korea	N=Total
14	15.0	5.0	0.0	35.0	0.0	45.0	(20)
15	9.0	4.5	13.6	18.1	22.7	31.8	(22)
16	4.5	9.0	9.0	41.0	22.7	13.6	(22)
17	20.0	0.0	6.6	53.3	20.0	0.0	(15)
18	17.7	0.0	5.8	39.4	11.7	35.2	(17)
19	5.8	0.0	5.8	41.1	23.6	23.6	(17)
20	11.1	3.7	14.8	37.0	22.2	11.1	(27)
21	6.6	16.6	10.0	20.0	23.3	23.3	(30)
22	0.0	36.0	24.0	16.0	16.0	8.0	(25)
23	3.3	13.3	10.0	6.6	6.6	30.0	(30)
24	0.0	6.0	12.1	15.1	15.1	24.2	(33)
25	0.0	3.3	16.2	29.0	29.0	19.3	(31)
26	0.0	6.6	20.0	20.0	20.0	16.6	(30)

Note: Volume year is from November to September, quarterly.

APPENDIX 15

DIVISION BY DISCIPLINE OF ARTICLES PUBLISHED IN THE JOURNAL OF ASIAN STUDIES
(all figures are percentages of N)

Volume	Anthropology	Art	Economics	Geography	History	Law	Literature & Language	Political Science	Sociology	Other	N=Total
14	5.0	0.0	20.0	0.0	40.0	0.0	15.0	0.0	10.0	10.0	(20)
15	0.0	4.5	13.7	0.0	18.1	0.0	9.0	22.8	18.1	13.7	(22)
16	0.0	0.0	18.1	4.5	13.7	0.0	13.7	13.7	22.7	13.7	(22)
17	6.6	6.6	0.0	0.0	20.0	6.6	13.3	20.0	6.6	20.0	(15)
18	0.0	0.0	11.7	0.0	41.1	0.0	5.8	5.8	17.6	17.6	(17)
19	0.0	0.0	17.6	11.7	58.8	0.0	11.7	0.0	0.0	0.0	(17)
20	0.0	0.0	3.7	7.4	33.3	0.0	0.0	33.3	18.6	11.1	(27)
21	[Unavailable]										(30)
22	16.0	4.0	4.0	0.0	44.0	0.0	4.0	4.0	28.0	4.0	(25)
23	3.3	3.3	10.0	3.3	40.0	3.3	6.6	20.0	10.0	3.3	(30)
24	20.6	0.0	0.0	0.0	41.3	0.0	3.4	17.2	10.3	6.8	(33)
25	6.4	3.3	9.6	3.3	45.1	3.3	12.9	16.2	0.0	0.0	(31)
26	10.0	0.0	6.6	3.3	66.6	0.0	3.3	6.6	0.0	3.3	(30)
Average	5.7	1.8	9.5	2.8	38.5	1.1	8.2	13.3	11.8		

CORRELATIONS OF AAS MEMBERSHIP INTERESTS WITH ARTICLES
PUBLISHED IN THE JOURNAL OF ASIAN STUDIES, 1957–1967

	Anthropology	Art	Economics	Geography	History	Language & Literature	Law	Political Science	Sociology
Professional Field	7.2	3.0	5.0	3.4	24.9	8.9	.9	19.1	3.2
Published Articles	5.7	1.8	9.5	2.8	38.5	8.2	1.1	13.3	11.8

Note: Figures are percentage averages of a twelve-year period (Vols. 14–26, with Vol. 21 unavailable). Averages of sample fields only.

	China	Japan & Korea	South Asia, incl. India	Southeast Asia.
Member Area Interest	22.2	15.4	13.8	14.4
Published Articles	34.4	19.1	27.4	12.5

Note: Figures are percentage averages of a ten-year period (1957–67). They do not include the areas of "General Far East," "East Asia," "Northeast Asia," and "Central Asia."

APPENDIX 17

AAS GENERAL FUND REVENUES AND DISBURSEMENTS, 1949-1969[a]

Year[b]	Revenues	Disbursements	Balance
1949	$ 8,539.92	$ 10,157.33	- 1,617.41
1950	10,001,86	8,453.62	1,548.24
1951	9,387.04	6,720.77	2,666.27
1952	8,877.39	9,451.23	- 573.84
1953	9,886.70	9,549.55	337.15
1954	9,511.53	8,661.23	850.40
1955	14,487.75	15,087.92	- 600.17
1956	20,097.59	11,984.22	8,123.37
1957	33,692.95	26,287.74	7,405.21
1958	35,032.81	28,704.74	6,328.55
1959	49,912.76	38,910.11	11,062.25
1960	54,766.82	44,099.51	10,669.31
1961	84,327.32	56,077.73	28,249.59
1962	90,295.89	75,157.99	15,137.90
1963	89,965.40	83,581.30	6,384.10
1964	101,095.83	111,676.37	- 10,580.54
1965	103,644.83	91,953.23	11,691.60
1966	115,743.61	97,606.55	18,137.06
1967	129,252.46	106,532.69	22,719.77
1968	129,015,76	128,085.04	930.13
1969	153,076.00	145,391.00	7,685.00

[a]Pre-1957 data are as complete as existing records can make them, but certainly incomplete.

[b]Fiscal year is same as calendar year.

APPENDIX 18

AAS REVENUES BY CATEGORIES, 1949-1969
(all figures are percentages)

	1969	1968	1967	1966	1965	1964	1963	1962	1961	1960	1959	1958	1957	1956	1955	1954	1953	1952	1951	1950	1949
Membership	39.7	39.8	37.7	36.9	26.7	24.5	23.8	22.2	19.3	31.8	27.6	22.9	20.2	30.4	41.7	45.9	43.9	50.5	44.2	39.1	42.4
New	(8.5)	(6.1)	(6.7)	(6.2)	(4.8)	(6.8)	(5.1)	(5.5)	(4.2)	(6.8)	(9.8)	(4.2)	(3.7)	...	(10.9)	(8.8)	(9.8)	(6.5)	(8.6)	(6.9)	(12.7)
Renewal	(31.2)	(33.6)	(31.0)	(30.7)	(21.8)	(17.6)	(18.7)	(16.7)	(15.2)	(25.0)	(17.8)	(18.7)	(16.4)	...	(30.7)	(37.0)	(34.0)	(44.0)	(35.7)	(32.2)	(29.6)
Journal	31.9	33.8	30.9	31.2	23.9	23.4	24.2	21.4	20.8	34.1	31.4	27.1	27.1	51.1	52.4	50.7	55.6	41.7	47.8	36.3	42.5
New, Institutional	(3.4)	(3.3)	(3.7)	(3.9)	(2.4)	(2.4)	(3.5)	(2.4)	(2.0)	(5.4)	(5.3)	(3.5)	(2.9)	...	(4.9)	(9.4)	(5.9)	(5.2)	(5.2)	(9.4)	(4.9)
New, Individual	(.01)	(.5)	(.1)	(.2)	(.2)	(.8)	(.3)	(.5)	(.5)	(.6)	(1.4)	(.6)	(1.1)	...	(4.6)	(1.8)	(1.2)	(.8)	(.7)	(.8)	(.3)
Renew. Instit.	(19.8)	(20.9)	(20.6)	(20.1)	(14.4)	(14.8)	(12.5)	(13.0)	(14.0)	(17.7)	(16.7)	(15.0)	(13.3)	(35.7)	(28.4)	(29.4)	(37.1)	(26.9)	(29.7)	(23.8)	(25.7)
Renew, Indiv.	(.001)	(.1)	(.1)	(.8)	(.2)	(.7)	(.5)	(.8)	(.5)	(1.7)	(.8)	(.7)	(1.7)	...	(1.2)	(1.2)	(.9)	(.5)	(1.2)	(.5)	(.7)
Single Copies	(1.4)	(2.8)	(.6)	(.4)	(1.1)	(1.3)	(2.9)	(1.0)	(1.2)	(2.3)	(1.7)	(1.3)	(2.9)	...	...	...	...	...	...	...	...
Bibliography	(.3)	(.3)	(.3)	(.4)	(.3)	(.4)	(.4)	(.6)	(.7)	(1.7)	(1.4)	(.6)	(.7)	...	(5.6)	(4.0)	(4.4)	(5.1)	(10.9)	(6.3)	(9.7)
Advertising	(6.9)	(5.7)	(5.3)	(5.2)	(5.1)	(3.0)	(4.0)	(2.9)	(1.7)	(4.6)	(3.9)	(3.6)	(3.5)	(10.7)	(6.3)	(4.0)	(3.4)	(2.1)	(1.8)	(1.7)	(1.1)
Misc.	...	...	...	...	...	...	...	...	...	...	...	(1.8)	(.8)	(4.7)	(1.5)	(1.4)	(2.6)	(.9)	(1.5)	...	...
Other	5.8	7.6	8.7	10.1	8.7	11.5	7.5	11.0	10.8	5.7	4.6	5.7	4.7	7.2	5.6	...	.5	.3	...	...	...
Interest	(3.7)	(5.6)	(7.0)	(10.0)	(7.3)	(10.2)	(6.9)	...	...	...	...	...	...	...	...	...	...	...	...	...	...
Dividends	(2.1)	(1.9)	(1.7)	(.1)	(1.4)	(1.3)	(.6)	...	...	...	...	...	...	...	...	...	...	...	...	...	...
Special Fund	22.6	18.7	22.6	21.6	14.5	13.7	14.2	15.3	16.9	19.6	21.9	18.3	13.9	11.1	.3	3.3	.1	...	7.9	18.3	15.1
Service Charges	(3.7)	(1.7)	(2.6)	(1.2)	(3.0)	(1.9)	(5.2)	(6.7)	(8.5)	(9.5)	(10.5)	(8.9)	(6.9)	...	...	...	...	...	...	(5.3)	...
Annual Meeting	(14.6)	(13.2)	(9.0)	(12.6)	(8.5)	(9.0)	(7.0)	(6.5)	(6.8)	(8.2)	(8.5)	(8.0)	(5.5)	...	...	(1.7)	...	...	...	...	...
Sale of Investments	(.4)	(.4)	(5.0)	(3.8)	...	...	...	...	...	...	...	...	...	...	...	...	...	...	...	...	...
Misc	(4.3)	(3.1)	(5.8)	(4.0)	(3.0)	(2.8)	(2.0)	(2.1)	(1.6)	(1.9)	(2.9)	(1.4)	(1.5)	...	...	(1.6)	...	...	...	(13.0)	...
Ford Operational	...	...	...	...	26.0	26.7	30.0	29.9	32.0	8.7	14.5	26.0	33.8	...	...	...	...	...	...	...	...
Ford Expansion	...	...	...	...	...	...	...	...	...	(5.0)	(9.5)	(18.9)	(18.9)	...	...	...	...	...	...	...	...
Ford Journal	...	...	...	...	...	...	...	...	...	...	(5.0)	(7.1)	(14.9)	...	...	...	...	...	...	...	...

APPENDIX 19

AAS DISBURSEMENTS BY CATEGORIES, 1949-1969
(all figures are percentages)

	1969	1968	1967	1966	1965	1964	1963	1962	1961	1960	1959	1958	1957	1956	1955	1954	1953	1952	1951	1950	1949
Journal	51.6	61.4	60.8	55.7	56.0	46.8	36.3	42.6	46.4	51.7	57.3	54.4	66.9	75.5	75.2	90.3	89.9	84.6	78.8	89.5	83.2
Publication	(26.5)	(34.0)	(30.2)	(31.0)	(28.5)	(26.9)	(20.8)	(32.1)	(38.4)	(42.2)	(36.9)	(33.3)	(44.0)	(73.5)	(72.9)	(85.1)	(78.2)	(84.6)	(78.8)	(89.5)	(83.2)
Editorial	(3.7)	(5.3)	(6.9)	(5.3)	(6.4)	(5.9)	(2.9)	(3.8)	(7.3)	(8.4)	(6.7)	(4.2)	(.9)	...	...	(1.5)	...	...	...	...	...
Bibliography	(21.4)	(22.0)	(23.7)	(18.9)	(21.0)	(13.9)	(12.5)	(6.6)	...	...	(11.4)	(12.8)	(18.9)	(2.0)	(2.3)	...	(3.1)	...	...	...	...
Reprints	...	...	...	...	...	...	...	...	(.7)	(1.1)	(.6)	(1.5)	(.7)	...	...	(3.7)	(8.5)	...	...	...	...
Misc.	...	...	...	...	...	...	...	...	...	...	(1.5)	(2.9)	(2.3)	...	...	...	...	...	...	...	...
Annual Meeting	8.0	8.6	7.7	8.8	6.4	6.8	6.1	6.4	7.3	7.7	7.2	7.3	5.7	...	.4	...	...	6.7	8.6	...	1.6
Newsletter	6.5	4.2	5.6	6.1	5.8	6.1	7.2	6.8	2.7	2.5	2.4	1.8	2.3	...	.4	...	...	...	...	...	...
Secretary	33.0	24.4	24.2	28.2	31.0	24.6	30.9	27.4	31.9	35.6	31.1	35.4	23.5	24.4	23.3	8.4	9.9	8.1	12.6	10.4	15.0
Salaries	(17.3)	(13.0)	(15.5)	(17.0)	(14.3)	(10.5)	(13.3)	(14.1)	(19.1)	(19.2)	(19.9)	(19.9)	(16.2)	...	...	...	...	...	(5.5)	(1.8)	(9.8)
Office	(10.0)	(6.1)	(3.5)	(5.6)	(4.8)	(4.2)	(3.4)	(4.6)	(4.7)	(5.1)	(3.3)	(4.3)	(3.3)	...	...	...	...	...	(1.6)	...	...
Telephone	(.4)	(.4)	(.4)	(.3)	(.4)	(.3)	(.4)	(.5)	(.5)	(.7)	(.9)	(.9)	(1.0)	...	...	...	...	...	...	(1.5)	(3.2)
Tax & Benefits	(2.4)	(1.1)	(.7)	(.8)	(.6)	(.3)	(.4)	(.5)	(1.0)	(1.0)	...	...	...	...	...	...	...	...	...	...	...
Depreciation	(.4)	(.5)	(.6)	(.6)	(.6)	(.4)	(.6)	(.6)	(.8)	(.8)	...	...	(.9)	...	...	...	...	...	...	...	...
Officer's Travel	(1.7)	(1.0)	(.7)	(.8)	(1.2)	(6.1)	(6.9)	(2.3)	(3.1)	...	(.5)	...	...	...	...	...	...	...	...	...	...
Other	(.5)	(2.1)	(2.8)	(3.1)	(8.9)	(2.6)	(5.8)	(4.7)	(2.7)	(8.7)	(6.4)	(10.3)	(2.0)	(24.4)	(23.3)	(8.4)	(9.9)	(8.1)	(5.5)	(7.0)	(2.0)
Treasurer's Office	.8	.2	1.4	1.1	.7	.5	.6	.9	1.5	1.1	2.0	1.1	1.3	...	.6	1.2	.2	...	...	...	...
Support Project-Committees	...	...	...	...	...	5.8	15.7	13.9	6.9	...	...	...	...	...	...	...	...	...	...	...	...
Taipei Center	...	...	...	...	...	6.7	...	...	...	...	...	...	...	...	...	...	...	...	...	...	...
Regional Meetings	...	...	...	...	...	2.6	3.1	1.9	3.2	1.4	...	...	...	...	...	...	...	...	...	...	...

APPENDIX 20

AAS SPECIAL FUND DISBURSEMENTS, 1957–1968

Year	Total (in $)
1957	45,714.92
1958	65,571.28
1959	75,965.44
1960	66.890.33
1961	132,805.40
1962	95,433.01
1963	104,800.35
1964	115,599.79
1965	93,800.39
1966	111,172.19
1967	282,639.89
1968	160,116.67

Note: Figures are per calendar year and represent total disbursement.

APPENDIX 21

AAS STOCKHOLDINGS AS OF DECEMBER 31, 1968

Stock	Year Acquired	Year Sold	Number of Shares	Additional Shares	Cost	Market Value[a]
Allied Chemical Company	1963	1966	400	8	$ 20,075.52	$ 19,647.05
Allied Stores Corporation	1968		200		$ 9,007.62	$ 7,750.00
American Electric Power, Inc.	1967		200		$ 7,927.26	$ 7,325.00
American Home Products Corp.	1968		100		$ 6,520.48	$ 5,862.50
American Telegraph & Telephone	1963	1966	200	10	$ 12,788.74	$ 12,446.40
Diamond Shamrock Company	1968		200		$ 6,922.26	$ 6.925.00
Dow Chemical	1967	1968	150		$ 9,920.58	$ 13,068.75
Ford Motor Company	1967		200		$ 9,258.88	$ 10,550.00
General Telephone & Electronics	1963	1966	300		$ 7,896.00	$ 13,251.30
Goodyear Tire & Rubber Co.	1967		200		$ 9,133.26	$ 11,075.00
Phelps Dodge Corporation	1967	1968	150		$ 10,802.41	$ 10,800.00
Southern Natural Gas Co.	1968		200		$ 9,786.50	$ 10,150.00
Standard Oil of Indiana	1967		200		$ 10,663.58	$ 12,200.00
Texaco, Inc.	1968		100		$ 8,034.49	$ 8,162.50

[a]Figures in this column represent market value as of December 31, 1968, <u>unless</u> sold.

INSTITUTIONAL CONNECTIONS OF MEMBERS OF THE AAS LEADERSHIP

Institutional affiliations of President, Secretary, Treasurer and Board of Directors through 1969. List is in rank order of number of times an institution has been repre-sented. In most cases, numbers represent same person being on Board, etc., more than once.

University of Michigan (19)
Harvard University (13)
Columbia University (11)
University of California, Berkeley (10)
Yale University (10)
University of Chicago (7)
Cornell (6)
University of Pennsylvania (5)
Syracuse (4)
Duke University (3)
Princeton University (3)
Stanford University (3)
University of Washington (3)
Library of Congress (2)
Massachusetts Institute of Technology (2)
Council on Foreign Relations
Institute of Pacific Relations
Freer Gallery
Japan Society
Nelson Gallery of Art (Kansas City)
Brooklyn College
Bryn Mawr
Colgate
Cheloo
Dartmouth
Haverford
Hawaii
Johns Hopkins
Northwestern
New York University
Ohio
Oberlin
University of Arizona
University of British Columbia
University of Florida
University of California, Los Angeles
University of Minnesota
University of Wisconsin

AAS MEMBERSHIP - LEADERSHIP CORRELATIONS
(all figures are percentages)

I. Leadership

Year	Social Science[a]	Humanities[b]	History	Other[c]	China	Japan	South Asia	Southeast Asia	Other[d]	S.S.	Human.	Hist.
	[Discipline]				[Area]					Unweighted Statistics; Leadership		
1969	44.8	5.2	50.0	...	37.9	12.0	29.4	15.5	5.2	50.0	4.2	45.8
1968	41.4	8.6	50.0	...	22.5	18.9	32.7	20.7	5.2	37.5	12.5	50.0
1967	43.1	12.0	44.8	...	32.7	27.6	24.1	15.5	...	45.8	12.5	50.0
1966	53.4	5.2	41.4	...	37.9	25.8	15.5	20.7	...	50.0	4.2	45.8
1965	58.6	5.2	36.2	...	34.4	29.3	13.8	22.5	...	62.5	4.2	33.3
1964	60.3	0.0	39.6	...	48.2	31.1	12.1	8.6	...	62.5	0.0	37.5
1963	60.3	5.2	34.5	...	46.5	32.7	17.2	3.4	...	54.1	4.2	41.7
1962	55.4	10.7	33.9	...	46.4	25.0	10.7	17.9	...	59.1	9.1	31.8
1961	50.0	12.5	37.5	...	23.2	35.7	19.6	21.4	...	45.5	13.6	40.9
1960	32.1	25.0	42.9	...	25.0	30.3	26.8	17.9	...	36.4	18.2	45.5
Ave:	49.9	8.9	41.1	...	35.5	26.8	20.2	10.7	...	50.3	8.3	38.4

II. Membership

Year	Social Science[a]	Humanities[b]	History	Other[c]	China	Japan	South Asia	Southeast Asia	Other[d]
1969	35.5	15.3	28.7	20.5	23.7	11.7	14.0	15.1	35.5
1968	38.4	15.4	28.9	17.3	24.8	12.5	14.3	15.6	32.8
1967	37.7	15.4	27.6	19.3	22.9	12.1	14.1	15.1	35.7
1966	39.1	16.4	27.2	17.3	22.1	12.6	14.8	15.6	34.8
1965	39.1	17.1	26.5	17.3	20.5	12.8	15.1	15.5	36.1
1964	39.9	16.3	25.0	18.8	20.1	12.8	14.4	14.9	37.8
1963	39.1	16.6	25.0	19.3	[Unavailable]				
1962	39.4	14.9	23.6	22.1	17.8	13.3	15.2	13.7	40.0
1961	40.5	15.6	24.0	19.9	18.3	13.2	15.4	13.5	39.6
1960	37.8	12.6	24.7	24.8	25.1	15.6	13.2	13.8	32.3
Ave:	38.6	15.6	26.1	19.7	21.7	12.5	13.9	14.7	36.0

[a] Social Science is defined as Anthropology, Economics, Geography, Journalism, Law, Political Science, and Sociology.

[b] Humanities is defined as Art, Language & Literature, and Philosophy & Religion.

[c] Other comprises miscellaneous membership categories such as Medicine, the physical and natural sciences, library work, and "unknown" (average: 14.5%).

[d] In the case of leadership, this area category is Korea. In the case of the membership statistics, this is defined as Far East, East Asia, Central Asia, Northern Asia, and other general geographic regions. It also includes "unknown."

Note: These statistics are intended to be suggestive rather than definitive, and thus should be interpreted with some caution. Leadership statistics are weighted to suggest degrees of influence in the policy-making process of the Association. Aside from the general problems inherent in such a device, it should also be noted that individual positions, depending on the persons filling them, are often less--or more--influential: e.g., an active president as opposed to an inactive one. Other factors which enter in are ones such as the high concentration of leadership of the Association in Ann Arbor (thus putting them closer to the "action"), and the problem of defining with precision the term leadership.

The leadership statistics are weighted according to the following:

President (5)	President Ex-Officio (1)
Secretary (4)	Treasurer (1)
Board Members (3)	Journal Editor (2)
Nominating Committee Chairman (2)	ACRD Chairman (1)
Program Committee Chairman (2)	Assistant Program Committee Chairman (1)
First Vice-President (1)	Publications Committee Chairman (1)
Second Vice-President (1)	

The total number of people involved in the AAS leadership thus defined is 24. With weighting, N=56 (1960-62) and N=62 (1963-69). Since ACRD Chairman and Publications Committee were added to the Executive Committee in 1963, and these two posts are occupied by someone already on the Board, they are weighted one (1) so as not to give them more weight than the President or Secretary.